(RE)CONSTRUCTING MEMORY, PLACE, AND IDENTITY IN TWENTIETH CENTURY HOUSTON

Dr Louis G. Mendoza

(RE)CONSTRUCTING MEMORY, PLACE, AND IDENTITY IN TWENTIETH CENTURY HOUSTON

A Memoir on Family and Being Mexican American in Space City USA

The Latinx Studies Collection

Collection editor
Dr Manuel Callahan

First published in 2023 by Lived Places Publishing

All rights reserved. No part of this publication may be reproduced, stored in a retrieval system, or transmitted in any form or by any means, electronic, mechanical, photocopying, recording or otherwise, without prior permission in writing from the publisher.

The authors and editors have made every effort to ensure the accuracy of information contained in this publication, but assume no responsibility for any errors, inaccuracies, inconsistencies and omissions. Likewise, every effort has been made to contact copyright holders. If any copyright material has been reproduced unwittingly and without permission the Publisher will gladly receive information enabling them to rectify any error or omission in subsequent editions.

Copyright © 2023 Lived Places Publishing

British Library Cataloguing in Publication Data

A CIP record for this book is available from the British Library

ISBN: 9781915271549 (pbk)

ISBN: 9781915271563 (ePDF)

ISBN: 9781915271556 (ePUB)

The right of Louis G. Mendoza to be identified as the Author of this work has been asserted by them in accordance with the Copyright, Design and Patents Act 1988.

Cover design by Fiachra McCarthy

Book design by Rachel Trolove of Twin Trail Design

Typeset by Newgen Publishing UK

Lived Places Publishing

Long Island

New York 11789

www.livedplacespublishing.com

Abstract

(Re)Constructing Memory, Place, and Identity in Twentieth Century Houston: A Memoir on Family and Being Mexican American in Space City USA tells the story of the Mendoza family over three generations as they navigate migrancy, social strata, and search for belonging in East Texas. Mendoza looks through the lens of community, family, and the self to identify connections between place, identity, and efforts to negotiate intense racialization in Texas and Houston, in particular. He addresses the challenges associated with reconstructing one family's narrative over three generations when extant family archives are limited. The book demonstrates how a coherent historical thread can be reconstructed through various literary and historical methods—primary and secondary sources, memory, oral histories, and creative non-fiction.

Key Words

Mexican American; memoir; Southwestern United States; ethnic identity; community; family; migration; oral history

Acknowledgments

I wish to thank The New College of Interdisciplinary Arts and Sciences at ASU's West Campus for a sabbatical in Fall 2022 that gave me the opportunity to complete this project. My siblings and extended family, my second cousins Rita Hernandez and John Mendoza, my aunt Gloria Mendoza and cousin Theresa Evenbly, my aunt Sister Patricia, and my partner, Angélica Afanador-Pujol, all contributed in various ways as readers, informants, and reviewers of the manuscript at various stages. Special thanks to Manolo Callahan, my editor at Lived Places Publishing who has been supportive, insightful, and a diligent reader. I am grateful to Lizmari Vasquez for her assistance in transcribing interviews, Emmanuel Ortiz for his assistance with the Bibliography section, and Haley Chance, librarian at St Thomas High School, for retrieving and scanning the yearbook for me from the school archives.

In memory of Joe Mendoza, Jr and Mary Concepción Martinez Mendoza

With love to

my dear siblings, Rosemary, Mary Ann, Bobby, Beabee, Margie, Cindy, and Gilda

and

my amazing partner Angélica Afanador-Pujol and my son Camilo Mendoza Afanador

Contents

Learning objectives	xiii
Prologue	xvii
Introduction	1
Chapter 1 Fragments of the past	15
Chapter 2 Becoming Americans	69
Chapter 3 Coming of age in the Space City	119
Coda	181
Notes	187
Recommended projects, assignments, and discussion questions	193
Bibliography	195
Index	209

Learning objectives

Introduction learning objectives: on historical perspective, genealogy, and historical methods

In this section of the book, students will learn the guiding principles, purposes, and methods for the exploration of familial and community history they are reading. These objectives will provide a road map for the book but also for any research they may wish to conduct.

- Historical perspective: Students will be able to understand how factors in a person's background, context, or experiences can shape the way they think and feel about a historical event.
- Genealogy: Students will gain an understanding of how their genealogy can provide them with a deeper understanding of their identity—where they came from, who they were, what they did, the challenges they overcame, the accomplishments they achieved, and the dreams they had.
- Historical methods: Students will gain insight into techniques, guidelines, and challenges associated with research and writing about the past.

Chapter 1 learning objectives: on causes of migration from Mexico in the early twentieth century

Students will be provided with an insight into the "push-pull" factors of Mexican migration to the United States in the early part of the twentieth century. This period led to a large Mexican diaspora to the north and an expansion of what came to be known as Greater Mexico.

Upon completion of this chapter, students will have an insight into the complex array of causes of migration, exile, and displacement of Mexicans from Mexico to the United States in the early twentieth century.

Chapter 2 learning objectives: on challenges faced by first-generation immigrants

This chapter will provide students with context for understanding a variety of social and cultural challenges faced by first-generation immigrants in school and in the workplace.

Upon completion of this chapter, students will have a stronger understanding of Americanization programs and processes, personal and communal resilience, and the impact of microaggressions in the workplace.

Chapter 3 learning objectives: the situated memoir as a form of bottom-up history

This learning objective asks the reader to consider how their own lives are part of a larger narrative, be it in the context of their familial, communal, regional, or national history. The questions below are intended to facilitate an exploration of your story. They are not intended to be comprehensive, but rather ask that you place your life story in relation to the world in which you live.

- How has your relationship to various social institutions shaped or contributed to your worldview?
- How have particular places impacted informed your identity?
- In what ways do neighborhoods either insulate or isolate its residents?
- Do you believe that personal memory is a reliable resource for constructing a story?
- Thinking though your life experience or that of a family member, identify epiphanic moments where one's place in society becomes clear and has led to social or political resistance or conformity. An epiphany is a visionary moment when someone has a sudden insight or realization that changes their understanding of themselves or their comprehension of the world.

Conclusion learning objectives: on applying learned knowledge

about constructing family histories

Through activities and reflection, students will learn to identify the strengths and limitations of various methods for recuperating family history and how they might proceed to use this model to recreate their own family's story.

Prologue

Memory's truth, because memory has its own special kind. It selects, eliminates, alters, exaggerates, minimizes, glorifies, and vilifies also; but in the end it creates its own reality, its heterogeneous but usually coherent version of events; and no sane human being ever trusts someone else's version more than his own — Salman Rushdie, *Midnight's Children*.

I was born in 1960 and raised in Houston, Texas. I thought of myself as Mexican American when growing up; only later did I realize that I was also a second-generation Mexican immigrant and that ethnic identifiers, what people call themselves, routinely change over time to reflect people's identity, politics, and their social and economic circumstances.[i] It was later when I came to understand that as a twentieth-century industrial city, the history of people of Mexican descent in Houston is uniquely "modern" when compared to other large cities of the southwest, especially those with a colonial past.

Like most people, my earliest childhood memories are kaleidoscopic in nature—fragmented and jumbled. Can they be made whole? To what end? To what extent does my perspective on my family's history resonate with others?

This project is motivated by my interest in recovering my familial history, which was rarely communicated in any coherent manner to my generation of siblings. While I knew that my paternal and maternal grandparents were immigrants from northern Mexico who came to the USA in pursuit of a better life for themselves and their progeny, little was ever conveyed to me about their pre-immigrant past or our familial ties in Mexico. According to a 2013 report from the Pew Foundation, my experience is not unusual for many second-generation immigrants.[ii] While many immigrants relocate to seek refuge from a difficult situation in their homeland, many do so with the idea that they will return home when the conditions that spurred their departure improve. This is especially true when their new destination is a neighboring country, and their country of origin is undergoing a difficult period that is expected to eventually pass. That expectation nurtures a hope that returning home is not only possible, but likely. *México de afuera* as an expatriate ideology emerged with particular force in the first quarter of the twentieth century, an intense era of displacement, exile, and migration from Mexico during which many migrants anticipated an imminent return home and strove to nurture their patriotism for the homeland. In this context, new immigrants often viewed their goal as recreating Mexican life in the United States. In this respect, according to Daniel Morales, a community of Mexican-descent people was but an extension of Mexico.[iii] But once an immigrant realizes that there will be no return home, either because of prolonged difficulties in the homeland or an unexpected acclimation to their new environment, their orientation becomes forward-looking and grounded in their current geo-location. They settle into jobs, begin raising a family, and develop familial and communal ties in the host country. In pre-high-tech eras without internet and international phone plans, when one lived a modest, working-class life, a return to one's nation of origin for a vacation or to maintain familial ties was rare and costly so maintaining a connection between family in the ancestral homeland and the new homeland was difficult. Thus, while certainly not literally, or even practically true, it often seemed to me that our history began and ended with the border. As a child, our extended family consisted of my grandparents, my parents, my seven siblings and myself, plus our huge extended family of 12 aunts and uncles and more than 70 first cousins. In the Prologue to *Historia: The Literary Making of Chicana and Chicano History*, a book on the relationship between literary and historical writing, I wrote the following paragraphs in memory of my grandparents and to acknowledge the limits of our relationship to them and their Mexican past. Additionally, I share other excerpts of life-writing, or creative non-fiction, that have informed my scholarship for more than three decades. Creative non-fiction imagines what life may have looked like for people in the context of their place and time. Historical fiction imagines what likely happened to real people without supporting documentation but accounting for the confirmed arc of historical events. The details and the events in the vignettes of creative non-fiction that follow directly below and in later chapters are a mix of actual events and imagined conversations designed to fill in gaps and provide emotional depth to our family's story.

***

When I was a child our large family's Sunday visits to our maternal and paternal grandparents were as regular as church. We tumbled out of the station wagon and paid homage to our grandparents, whose small houses smelled like the inside of a cedar chest and were as neat and clean as they were dark and cool. The visits always started off formally with a ritual hug, kiss, and pinch of the cheek followed by a survey of our appearance. Were we clean? Groomed? Eating well? Well-behaved?

We kids marveled at how these small two-bedroom wood-frame houses had managed to hold our parents' larger families of six and nine children respectively. Invariably, after our grandparents asked us how school was going in their halting English, the conversation between grandma and grandpa and mom and dad would take place almost exclusively in Spanish. Sometimes we stayed listening in amazement at how they could understand each other when it seemed everyone was talking as fast as they could all at the same time.

Grandma and grandpa on both sides of the family spoke little English despite having lived in Texas the vast majority of their lives. Driven from their home country of Mexico by the quest for a better life and a civil war that lasted much of the first three decades of the twentieth century, the USA seemed to promise economic opportunity and safety. My grandparents arrived in Texas sometime between 1903 and 1924. Fifty and sixty years later they could look back without regret upon their lives of work, of survival, of hardship, of tenacity, and, yes, of dignity and progress despite an often unwelcome social and political climate. Though I know they loved us, their children's children, dearly, our relationship was mitigated by our mutual language limits. Separated from them by only a generation, our first language was English. So, it was that we moved among them with respect, a respect not unlike our Catholicism, borne of fear and love—undergirded by these qualities, our relationship was also limited by our ignorance of the particulars of their lives.

Years later I would wonder how they felt about this generational shift, this language gap that existed between us. Did they think us sell-outs, cultural misfits, as a tragic consequence of assimilation, or did they foresee that cultural characteristics like language would be the price we paid for "Americanization," for "progress?" From my perspective as a child, I saw them as a link to an archaic past, one that I did not fully understand yet nevertheless knew I should revere. And despite not being able to share the details of our lives with them, I sensed that we pleased them, and that they loved us unconditionally despite our language differences. (*Mendoza, 2003*).

***

My parents, Mary Martinez (1927) and Joe Mendoza (1928), experienced not only the economic hardship of the Depression, but the 1930s era of Mexican deportation and the suspicion of being un-American that everyone, but especially those who were "foreign-looking," faced when they participated in labor strikes or stood in line for government assistance. The Catholic schools my parents attended in East Houston forbade them to speak Spanish under the threat of corporal punishment or some other form of humiliation. Intimidated, they often suffered in silence. My mom tells the story of how even in high school, despite the fact that she was one of the few graduates in her family, she was so shy about speaking in public that she would ask the teacher if her friend, Mary Escalante, could read her work for her rather than suffer the embarrassment of having her accent "corrected" in front of the class.

Even now I cringe when I think of how 25 years later the nuns at Resurrection Elementary where Mary and Joe (the Spanish language versions of their names had long ago been anglicized) sent their children, practiced the same pedagogy. I recall classmates being forced to stand in front of class every afternoon and practice saying "chair," "church," "chicken,'" "children,'" "shutters,'" "shine your shoes,'" and so on, so they could improve their enunciation of English and eradicate their Spanish accent. (Mendoza, *2005*)

***

Interstate 10 slices through Denver Harbor like a swollen scar of an improperly cared for wound. Railroad tracks surround it-— they are the sutures holding our wounds together. The healing process is never-ending. People are contained within by the less visible barriers of poverty and comunidad. In our house on Zoe Street, I used to lie awake at night in one of the upstairs bedrooms my father and his compadres had added on to better house our large family. There, the painful squeaks and moans of rusty freight cars passing in the night would sing me to sleep. Those eerie sounds both haunted and tempted me. They seemed to call, to dare me to hop on and take off to new, unknown places. Their motion was persistent—-shhh, shhh, shhh, all roads lead out shh, shh, shh, they whispered. In the dark, in my bed, I let them take me away to happier, unreal places. During the day these cumbersome caterpillars crawled rudely through our world. Doug, Larry, and I used to wait for them on Wallisville or Old Clinton Road—out of defiance we jumped on them, only to hop off after a few blocks. The ride was always disappointing, falling far short of our expectations. *(Mendoza, 2003*

Knowledge of my family's history was also kaleidoscopic in nature—not known with any certainty beyond that facts that both sets of grandparents had come in the first quarter of the twentieth century from northern Mexico. *(Re)Constructing Memory, Place, and Identity in Twentieth Century Houston* is premised on the idea that neither my experiences nor my limited knowledge about my past is unique, that this dissonance with my past is a result of twin pressures: my family's need to look forward and educational policies that sought to provide a master narrative of the state and nation that homogenized our experiences, flattened, or eradicated our differences, and built a consensus narrative that elided conflict or injustice, rather than reflect a past that was, in reality, complex, and often conflicted.

This book seeks to explore the interconnectedness of place and ethnic identity in the emergence of Houston's Mexican American community through the lens of one family's experience. Thus, it is at once communal, familial, and personal. The book also addresses the challenges associated with piecing together one family's narrative over three generations as a representative framework for understanding change, social transformation over time, and the role of memory, as well as its limitations, in crafting one's story. Using a combination of archival resources, oral histories, and secondary sources, I intend to convey the story of the Mendoza and Martinez families over three generations as they navigated migration from northern Mexico, social and economic challenges, and searched for and built a new home and a sense of belonging in east Texas.

Every time one writes (his)stories based on "truth," one (re)creates a representation of a memory, dream, wish, or desire of an actual event as one remembers or interprets it. I don't believe there is a singular absolute truth that suits everyone's reality or experience. Nor do I believe that what we call history is necessarily truer than what we call fiction even if the former proposes to be grounded in "truth," "reality," or "facts." The perspective of the writer matters. Memory is never pure, unbiased, or even neutral.

This is one family's story over time. Mine. That does not mean that all of my family members would claim this to be their story in the same way I do. I respect that. Even though my siblings' memories inform this story, ultimately the book is the perspective of one family member who seeks to create a concise and coherent narrative to represent three generations of his family's experiences. I am not a historian, a sociologist, or an anthropologist. As a literary and cultural critic, I am an analyzer and crafter of words. I admire the power of language, the skill it takes to tell a good story, the power of story to inform, motivate, and inspire us, to soothe and arouse us, to give us cause to reflect, dream, or rouse us to action. Each of the above academic disciplinary practitioners also believe in and practice storytelling using methodologies that gather data to tell a story. Each in their own way has a different relationship to facts, data, memory, and truth. In many respects, *(Re)Constructing Memory, Place, and Identity in Twentieth Century Houston* borrows, utilizes, and blends those methods while also adding an element of creative non-fiction to fill in gaps and convey a slightly more comprehensive picture as possible of what my family's life, past and present, may have looked and felt like. And yet, even as I acknowledge the limited perspective I offer, I hope that this story resonates with others.

A transborder backstory

In this section, I explore my family history in Mexico and seek to establish a context for their migration *al norte*. The Mendoza and Martinez family stories that precede our immediate grandparents are ones that I have recovered only while working on this book. I have often wondered about these unknown ancestors, where they lived, what their lives were like, and what motivated them to leave their ancestral homes. I have often felt that one's sense of self is deeply imbricated in one's geographic location. The interconnectedness of genealogy and geography is not happenstance, but rather a portal into understanding the workings of culture and everyday life.

In my father's small home office were three very old, beautifully framed large photographs of austere looking people. I was told that these were my father's maternal grandfather from Mexico, who he had no memory of ever meeting; his mother as a very young woman; and a 1924 wedding photo of his parents. He had inherited the photos from his mother when she died in the early 1980s. In their photos, his father and mother were both dressed formally—he in a suit and she in a lace dress. These photographs were some of the very few artifacts I had of a great grandparent from Mexico and of my grandparents as a young couple in the first quarter of the twentieth century.

A few weeks of research on Ancestry.com was revealing. I learned that my father's grandfather on his mother's side was Irineo Olvera, spouse of Adelaida Cano Olvera, both from Parras de la Fuente in Coahuila, Mexico. From birth certificates, baptism records, death records, and marriage certificates, I learned much more about these great-grandparents and others. Below I share partial results

Image 1 José and María Mendoza wedding photo, 09/17/1924.

Prologue xxvii

From Mendoza family archives

by way of family trees that began with my parents. What we will see is that I have been able to uncover my genealogical roots quite extensively in some areas with lesser results in others. I begin with my paternal grandfather for brevity and ease.

José Mendoza, my paternal grandfather, was born in 1891 in Cedros, Zacatecas to Nicolás Mendoza and Tomasa García. This

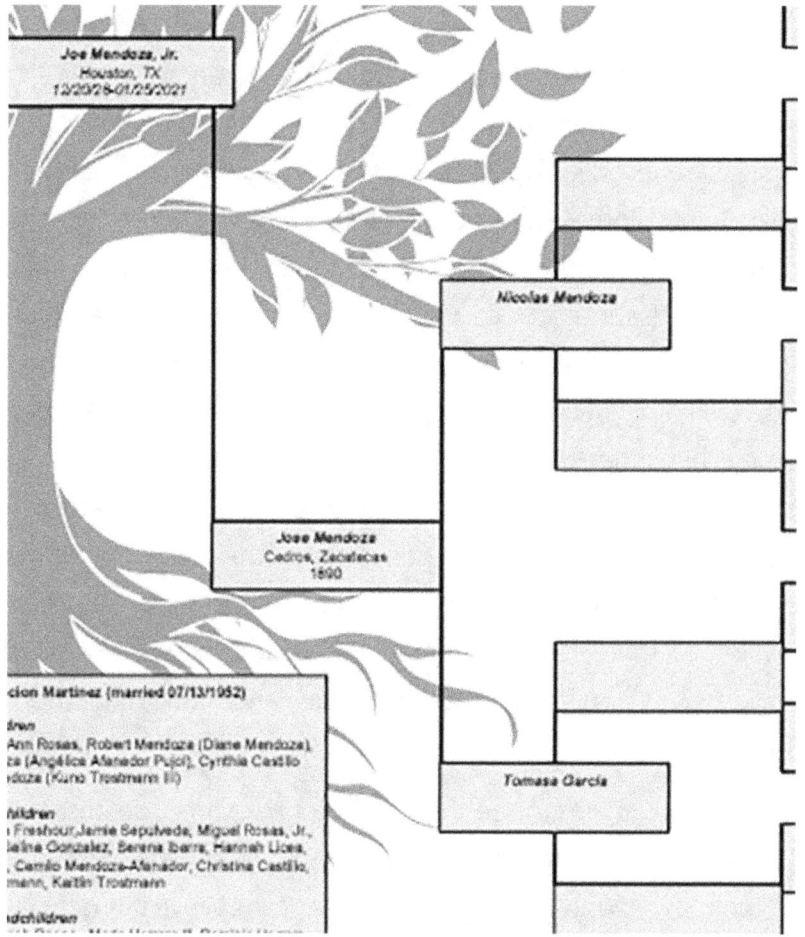

Image 2   José Mendoza lineage family lineage (2022).

information was obtained from the marriage certificate issued in 1924 when he and my grandmother Maria J. Olvera were married in Houston at Our Lady of Guadalupe Church in Houston's Second Ward. For reasons I will explain in the next chapter, I have been unable to locate any additional information about his parents.

I had better luck researching records on my father's mother and her family. For several generations going back as far as the late eighteenth century, it appears that my grandmother's maternal ancestors resided in or near Parras de la Fuente in Coahuila, although a great-great-great-grandfather of mine, José Antonio Casmiro Cano, was born in Ciudad Altamirano, Guerrero in 1784. Thus, the union of my father's grandmother's maternal grandparents was a result of a migration northward of more than 1,400 kilometers by José Antonio. Records reveal that the family of Felix Martinez, my mother's father, lived in various small municipalities in north of Monclova in Coahuila. He was born in Escobedo, about 185 miles north of Parras de la Fuente and approximately 512 kilometers from Teocaltiche, Jalisco, Mexico where his father Luis Martinez was born. It thus appears that some ancestors were moving northward in the mid-nineteenth century. Going back eight generations, the recovery of my maternal grandmother's family history is the most extensive. While the more recent generations resided in the Monclova region of Coahuila, eighteenth-century ancestors came from Tamaulipas.

What does it mean to see the records of marriages, deaths, and births? Many members of both sides of my family were practicing Catholics who underwent the rite of baptism. While it is difficult to discern facts of their everyday lives, such as their economic

Prologue xxix

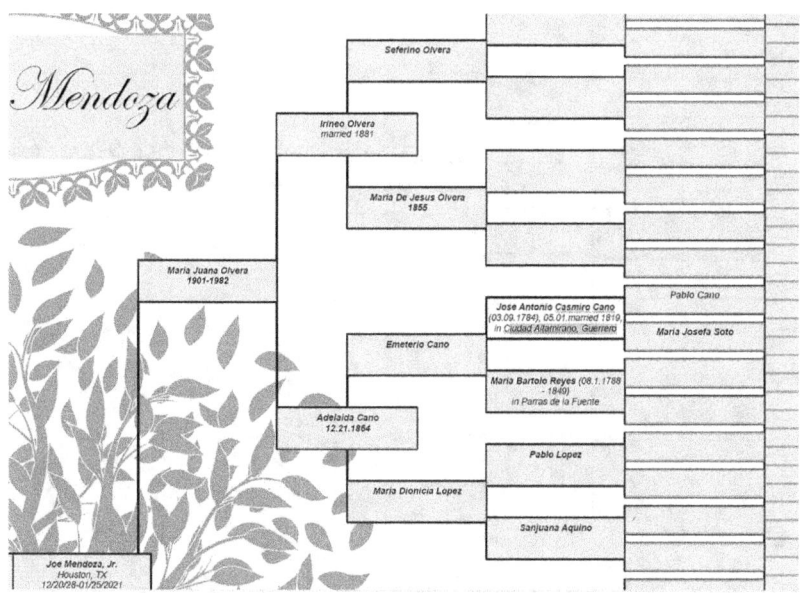

Image 3   María Olvera Mendoza family lineage (2022)

Image 4   Map of Southern Mexico from the city of Zihuatanejo in the State of Guerrero

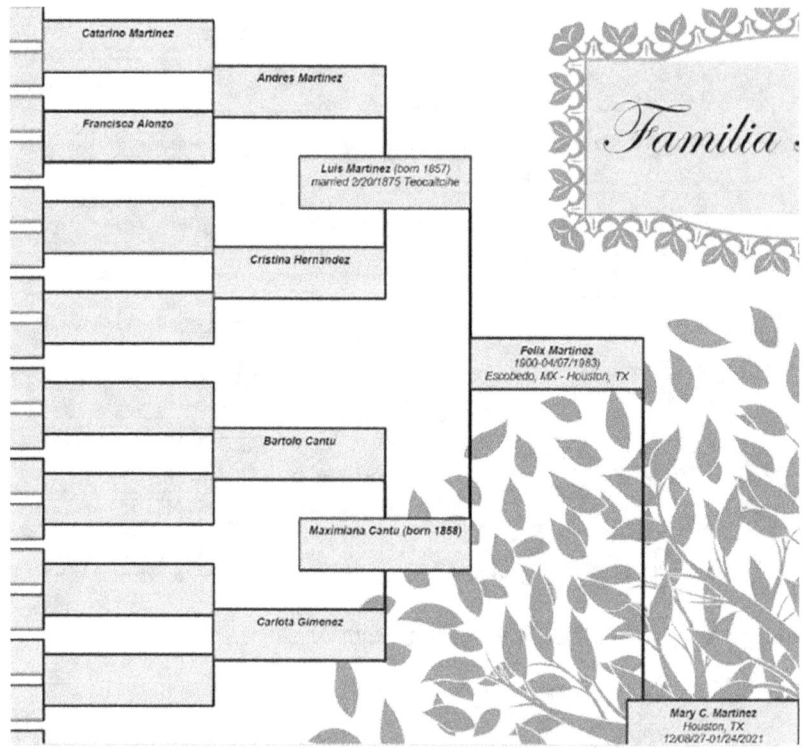

Image 5   Felix Martinez Family lineage (2022).

status or occupations, it is also clear that life was fragile and death of children or women in childbirth was not at all uncommon. One can surmise that they did not lead lives of luxury. Migration within Mexico was most likely motivated by a search for better living conditions. Stability in a region likely meant that sustenance and living conditions were sufficient enough to provide food, shelter, and a sense of community for the family. I cannot know with certainty what life in these small villages entailed for my ancestors. I can imagine, however, that they were immersed in the local economy as agricultural workers, or engaged as miners, or employed on a hacienda as *peones*. I can also surmise what it

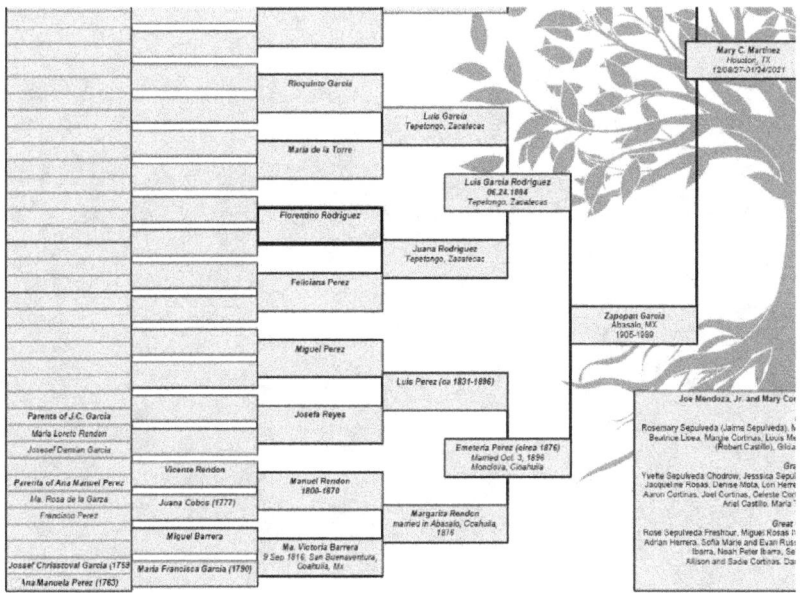

Image 6   Zapopan García family lineage (2022)

must have meant to uproot themselves and leave their homeland in the first part of the twentieth century.

As I begin tracing their journeys to Houston in the early twentieth century, I will try to recreate the circumstances which led to the profound, and no doubt difficult, decision to migrate *al norte*. While I do not have the benefit of many documents or first-hand accounts in my grandparents' words, I will utilize scholarship, familial oral histories, and creative non-fiction to portray their stories.

Introduction

Unlike San Antonio, Los Angeles, Tucson, Santa Fe, St. Augustine, or even New Orleans the history of Houston is not steeped in a Spanish or Mexican colonial past. Yet as the fourth largest city in the United States, as of 2021 the Houston Metropolitan Statistical Area (MSA) included 2.7 million Latinos, meaning that this region has the fourth largest Latino population in the country. While the San Antonio MSA includes 54.7 percent Latinos, the actual number of the Latino population in San Antonio is only slightly less than 25 percent of the number of Latinos residing in Houston's MSA.[i] Following only Chicago and Los Angeles, Houston has the third largest number of Mexican immigrants in the country.

When compared to the city of San Antonio, which was founded in 1718, Houston's development follows a very different trajectory. The land upon which the city of Houston was built, was purchased by brothers John Kirby Allen and Augustus Chapman Allen in August 1836, a mere four months after the decisive Battle of San Jacinto on April 21st in which the Texian army led by General Sam Houston defeated the army led by Mexican President and General Antonio López de Santa Anna. Santa Anna was captured the next day and many of his solders executed. Under duress the Mexican army retreated south of the Rio Bravo and Santa Anna was released following the signing of the Treaty of Velasco in which he recognized Texas's independence in exchange for his freedom.[ii] The Allen brothers named the city after their friend,

Sam Houston. One might say, then, that the city of Houston arose from the ashes of a successful rebellion by Anglo colonists and Tejanos against Mexico.

In November of that year, at a special joint session of Texas's Congress, the city of Houston was elected as the state capital. The Allen brothers had deliberately selected the land upon which Houston was built because it was where White Oak and Buffalo Bayous converged; the contemporary name for this place of convergence, Allen's Landing, bears the name of the brothers. Their intention was to create a town that could benefit from proximity to the Galveston waterway; their short-term goal was to have it named the capital of the new state of Texas. In their August 1836 advertisement appealing to potential settlers they noted:

> Nature appears to have designated this place for the future seat of Government. It is handsome and beautifully elevated, salubrious and well-watered, and now in the very heart or centre of the population, and will be so for a length of time to come. It combines two important advantages: a communication with the coast and foreign countries, and with the different portions of the Republic. (McComb, D.G., 1969)

When the first steamship ever to visit Houston arrived in January 1837, the town totaled 12 residents and one log cabin. Four months later there were 1,500 people and 50 houses. Houston did serve as the temporary capital of the Republic of Texas, but the heat, humidity, and mosquitoes discouraged support for it becoming the permanent site of the state capitol.

When established, the charter of the city called for it to encompass nine square miles with the courthouse in the center and two aldermen to be elected from each of four wards. Eventually fifth and sixth wards were also established (McComb, 72).

From the outset, Houston was steeped in the dynamics of racism. An active slave market operated out of downtown and in the years immediately prior to the Civil War, according to the 1860 census, the number of registered slaves in the city had doubled (Jackson, 1980). In the aftermath of the Civil War, Houston became a well-integrated city for a while. An 1870 population table by McComb showing racial distribution by wards reveals that the wards had a healthy balance of African Americans and Anglos in each ward with Fifth Ward having a slight majority of African Americans. It was not until the early part of the twentieth century that Jim Crow laws were completely enacted and enforced at the neighborhood level, even though the post–Civil War era was rife with the enactment of a number of formal and informal laws and regulations that restricted access to full citizenship, economic opportunity, and mobility. Among these were separate schools for "coloreds," separate passenger cars on trains, separate streetcars, separate waiting areas in railroad stations, a poll tax, miscegenation laws, separate libraries, separate health care facilities for the care of tuberculosis, separate bus seating, separate use of pools and water fountains, and support for the separation of races in places like movie theaters.

Houston did not attract Mexicans or Tejanos as a place to settle in the nineteenth century. In fact, the population of Mexicans shrunk before it grew. Throughout most of the nineteenth century most Mexican immigrants traveled to the Rio Grande

Valley, El Paso, and San Antonio; they did not go to east Texas cities like Houston. Anglos in east Texas had imported southern culture and racial attitudes, thus they preferred sharecroppers who were African American and Anglo. Robert R. Treviño, author of *The Church in the Barrio: Mexican American Ethno-Catholicism in Houston*, said that the Anglos "made it clear that Mexicans were not welcome." (2006)

According to Jesus Esparza, in the immediate aftermath of the defeat of General Santa Anna's forces in 1836, "Texians (Anglo Texans) ordered Mexican prisoners to clean the swampland on which Houston would be built. Afterwards, most would be sent home, but many stayed, creating the starting point of early Mexican settlement in the Houston region." (2011) Perhaps because of this auspicious beginning, unlike communities along the border or San Antonio which had a sizable and long-standing Mexican presence, Houston did not become a destination of choice for Tejanos or incoming Mexican migrants in the nineteenth century. At various points between 1850 and 1880, 6 to 18 Mexicans lived in Houston. Treviño asserts that "Mexicans were almost invisible in Houston during most of the nineteenth century." (2006) Nestor Rodriguez, author of "Hispanic and Asian Immigration Waves in Houston," writes that the 1880 US census showed only a "handful" of Mexicans in Houston. (2000) According to Santillan et al., that census counted fewer than ten persons of Mexican ancestry within the municipal boundaries. (2017) Esparza also notes that "Between 1836 and 1900, Mexicanos lived on the outskirts of Houston coming in to town mostly to find work." Many worked in unskilled labor and as food vendors. By 1900, 500–1,000 people of Mexican origin lived in Houston.

By 1900, Mexican migrants began to settle permanently within the city, occupying a region southeast of downtown called the Second Ward (Segundo Barrio), which quickly became the unofficial hub of their cultural and social life. Things were soon to change with the pull of employment opportunities catalyzed by the industrial revolution and the push of social unrest in Mexico as they inched toward civil war. In Houston, the need for laborers was particularly strong in the shipping and railroad yards. Propelled from their homes by the hardships of the Díaz modernization program and the danger and chaos of the Mexican Revolution, many *mexicanos* fled north using the railroads to travel to Texas and they gravitated toward where good jobs could be found.

Houston comes of age as a twentieth century city. The emergence of Houston as an industrial city and major urban center occurs simultaneously with the growth of the city's Mexican and larger Latino population. Unlike other major metropolitan areas in the country, comparatively few scholarly studies have been written about Houston, with even fewer focusing on the Mexican-descent population. With the exception of scholars such as Arnoldo De León, Robert Treviño, Arturo Rosales, Thomas Kreneck, Tyina Steptoe, and a few others, most historians of Houston have neglected focusing on Houston's Mexican community. Most attention to the experience of Tejanos has been focused on South Texas, the borderlands of El Paso, or the city with the oldest colonial presence in Texas, San Antonio. This book seeks to complement De León and Treviño's work by offering a bottom-up perspective of a single family that I see as relatively representative of the vast majority of this community's experiences. This book does not privilege the perspective of an exceptional politician, grassroots leader, or of an industry giant. Rather, what I seek in offering my family's story is discovery and connection, and familial idiosyncrasy and common ground, both of which express the challenge of recovering one's own past as well as demonstrating how each life matters as part of a collective.

In the early twentieth century Houston's population of Mexican descent increased due to several factors. The 1910 Mexican Revolution drove many Mexicans to Houston. Employers recruited Mexican Americans and made them into *enganchadores* (labor agents) so that they could recruit more workers; the *enganchadores* recruited Tejanos from other parts of the state and from immigrants. Mexican Americans in rural areas throughout Texas faced unemployment as commercial agriculture increased, and thus were willing to relocate to Houston since its economy was thriving. The labor shortage during World War I especially encouraged Mexicans to seek work in Houston. The increased work demands from the building of the Houston Ship Channel, the continued development of railroad infrastructure in the area, and agricultural work in areas around Houston likely had as much influence as the Mexican Revolution did in Mexicans relocating to Houston. Growth of the Mexican population was consistent. In 1920 Houston had 6,000 residents of Mexican origin. In 1930 about 15,000 residents were of Mexican origin. (The Texas Politics Project, "Population Growth in Texas, 1850–2000")

Tyina Steptoe notes in her important book that "Between 1920 and the end of the twentieth century, Houston transformed from a town with the forty-fifth largest population in the United States into the nation's fourth largest city. In the process, Houston transitioned from a society with an Anglo and African American racial dynamic into a multiethnic/multiracial metropolis." (2016) Steptoe's work shows how multiple groups migrating to Houston in the twentieth century impacted Houston's sense of space and race. She asserts that there was not a single Black identity, just as there was not a single ethnic Mexican identity in the interactions between *Tejanos* and Mexican nationals. Steptoe argues that the "… creation of the wards in Houston affected how neighborhoods developed, and how the racial communities emerged."In the early part of the twentieth century, the era of integration was over and even though wards stopped being recognized as geopolitical units in 1905, Steptoe argues that "these districts still shaped how Houstonians made sense of the city until after WWI." (2016) Numerous policies and practices conspired to limit and influence population distribution in Houston. Everything from lending practices to educational polices to zoning regulations and transit systems began instituting limits and developing color lines that regulated where people could live. Having grown up in Denver Harbor in the '60s and '70s, a neighborhood whose boundaries were defined by railroad tracks on all four sides and cut in half by Interstate 10, it was easy to see which neighborhoods had a mixture of manufacturing industries, refineries, warehouses, landfills, and workers relative to middle and upper class inner-city and suburban communities of white-collar professionals.

Magnolia Park, an unincorporated community on the eastern edge of Houston, began to attract Mexican immigrants in the late 1910s and early 1920s as the Ship Channel developed. As time passed, Mexicans began moving to other neighborhoods, such as the First Ward, the Sixth Ward, the Northside (then a part of the Fifth Ward), and Magnolia Park. A group of Mexican families also settled in the Houston Heights. By 1910, Houston's Mexican descent population was 2,000 (Rosales, 1981). Treviño notes that growth of the Mexican population grew steadily after the turn of the century. In 1907 a *junta patriótica* (cultural committee) launched the local Mexican Independence Day festivities. By 1908 at least one Mexican American mutual aid society had formed. (De León, 1989)

Goals and structure of the book

This book explores the interconnectedness of community, family, and the self to illustrate the interplay between place, identity, and racialization in Texas and Houston, in particular. Throughout this book, I identify the challenges associated with piecing together one family's narrative over three generations when traditional resources of family archives are limited. It will thus explore the reconstruction of a coherent historical thread through various literary and historical methods—primary and secondary sources, memory, oral histories, and creative non-fiction. In each chapter I will establish a context for the development of the city, the continuing rise of the Mexican-descent population, and the location of my family in Houston's context with as much attention as possible to specific dynamics that shaped their daily lives.

Prior to outlining the substance of each chapter, I should note the complex nature of identity for immigrant communities in an urban context. Arnoldo De León, author of *Ethnicity in the Sunbelt*, notes that a common feature of books by Chicana/

o urban historians has been a desire "to explain the process of institutionalized subordination." It was also important, he states, to demonstrate "how Chicanos created constructive responses to the forces they faced. The urban setting was a place where Mexican Americans lived in a familiar surrounding and where they could both identify with the traditions of the homeland while accepting tenets of the host society on their own terms." (1989) These dynamics were operable in Houston to be sure. Unlike other cities with a longer legacy of control and social, economic, cultural, and political power by people of Mexican descent, in Houston, ethnic Mexicans faced numerous challenges and much resistance to their efforts for individual and collective advancement. Yet, those struggles are not central to this narrative. Nor is this project invested in identifying a legacy of leaders, though there were many over the years. Rather, what I seek to do is use my family's experiences as a gauge for how "everyday" people negotiated the complexities of their circumstances to survive and sometimes thrive.

We were a family or *norteños*. While there were certainly distinctions between us as Tejanos and the people of Northern Mexico from which we hailed, it was always clear to us that our cultural touchstone was Northern Mexico. In our preference for flour tortillas over corn tortillas, and our embrace of *canción ranchera, corridos, cumbias,* and polka we connected with our Mexican cultural traditions and extended them to our Tejano reality. Yet, as Tejanos and immigrants, our familial presence in this land did not precede the US Mexican War. With non-English speaking parents, my parents likely remained cognizant of their status as first-generation immigrants. However, despite our almost monolingual grandparents, my siblings and I had no doubt that we were Americans of Mexican descent as well as Tejanos. Whatever experiences of racialization we had to varying degrees, they were experienced from that perspective, whether we felt marginalized, enraged, or even confused.

Chapter 1, "Fragments of the past: on family genealogy as a mosaic," will tell the story of my maternal and paternal grandparents' migration to Texas from Northern Mexico in the first quarter of the twentieth century. My grandparents were part of the migration phenomenon that occurred when Mexicans seeking to flee the violence and instability of the Mexican Revolution in the turn of the twentieth century were enticed to the United States to take advantages of the opportunities produced by the rapid growth in the railroad, shipping, agricultural, manufacturing, building, and oil industries. Initially entering the workforce as migrant farmworkers in the cotton fields of Texas or as day laborers, my grandfathers became a bricklayer and a shipyard dock worker when they settled down in Texas to raise their families. Houston is a decidedly twentieth-century Latino city. Unlike San Antonio, the Rio Grande Valley, or El Paso, Houston did not grow into an industrial town of significant size until the industrial revolution and Mexican migration both occurred.

As with many descendants of working-class migrants, archives and documentation are scant. I will draw on familial memory and secondary sources that depict the lives of working-class *mexicanos* in Houston. My grandparents eventually settled four city blocks from each other and raised large families of six and nine children. I will utilize a few family documents, like marriage licenses, birth certificates, and photographs alongside oral histories collected from immediate and extended family members about my grandparents' life in Mexico, their transition to the USA and their maintenance, however fragile, of ties to Northern Mexico. Some part of the story will be told through creative non-fiction to fill in gaps, to dramatize certain incidents, and to try to imagine the emotions that surely must have been at play in these times of change.[iii]

Chapter 2 "Becoming Americans: surviving, negotiating, and thriving under acculturation" focuses on my parents' stories. Born in the late 1920s, my parents, José Mendoza, Jr and María Concepción Martínez, were children of the Great Depression and the accompanying period of intense anti-foreigner sentiment and concomitant Americanization of that era. They grew up just a few blocks away from one another on Canal Street in Magnolia Park, one of the oldest Mexican neighborhoods of Houston. When they married in the early 1950s and moved to a nearby neighborhood, the one where I was sixth-born in 1960, they were one of the first ethnic Mexican American families in the neighborhood and the first on their block. By the time I was pre-teen, white exodus from the inner city transformed the demographics of our neighborhood so it was majority ethnic Mexican. In many respects, this was a phenomenon that characterized the transformation of the inner city and the development of the suburbs resulting from post–World War II GI Bill redlining by the banks and the housing industry. In this and many ways, I believe my family experience exemplifies that of Mexican-descent Houston. In the early 2010s, I recorded eight hours of oral history interviews with my parents about their lives. Using their story as a foundation, I wish to tell how their story can be seen as a typical story of first-generation Mexicans in Houston. To the extent possible, even as I tell the life stories of my parents and grandparents, I want to not lose sight of the social-political-cultural context of their lives. While we did not wield political or economic power, I believe my parents modeled what we now call cultural citizenship—that is a strong and engaged connection and commitment to their community and church, which, alongside their belief in the value of education as a vehicle for social mobility, they believed was sufficient to achieve the "American Dream." According to Renato Rosaldo:

> Cultural citizenship refers to the right to be different (in terms of race, ethnicity, or native language) with respect to the norms of the dominant national community, without compromising one's right to belong, in the sense of participating in the nation-state's democratic processes. The enduring exclusions of the color line often deny full citizenship to Latinos and other people of color. From the point of view of subordinated communities, cultural citizenship offers the possibility of legitimizing demands made in the struggle to enfranchise themselves. These demands can range from legal, political, and economic issues to matters of human dignity, well-being, and respect. (1994)

Facing extreme pressure to Americanize and to not draw undue attention to themselves, like many others in working-class barrios throughout the country, my family put their heads down, worked hard, took note of who their allies and antagonists were, participated actively in neighborhood institutions, and advanced familial and personal goals as active and engaged members of their community.

Chapter 3, "Coming of age in the Space City: cowboys, astronauts, and other specters" will transition to my own coming of age memoir, not because I believe my story is exceptional, but because I believe there are many elements of my story, experiences, and relationships that are representative of untold segments of Houston and Chicano youth history in general. Vivian Gornick asserts that "… memoir is a work of sustained narrative prose controlled by an idea of the self under obligation to lift from the raw material of life, a tale that will shape experience, transform events and deliver wisdom." (2002) This book seeks to render a story that deserves to be told.

My story will describe what it means to be one of eight children in a tight-knit extended family and an emerging inner-city barrio in which poor whites and Chicanos forged close relationships even as numerous racial tensions coexisted. My story is shaped by influences that are typical of many youths: family, neighborhood, church, school, and media, but within Chicanx/Latinx youth literature very few stories are written about Houston as a site of identity formation.

The Coda will lay the groundwork for a sequel to the author's own story as he undergoes a process of political and social conscientization that is parallel to his education—both as a worker, then college student, then professor. It will review key struggles in the effort to reconstruct a family genealogy where few traditional resources exist.

1
Fragments of the past: on family genealogy as a mosaic

José Mendoza, circa 1903

Thirteen-year-old José woke up, as he always did, when the roosters began to crow outside the *taller de hojalata* where he slept. It was still dark, but the roosters were sensitive to the break of dawn and crowed each morning only minutes before sunlight broke the horizon and gave shape to his dark surroundings. It was hard to imagine a different life. Here he had a roof over his head, he was learning to work with his hands, and he never went hungry. But the offer made to him yesterday, to travel to *los estados unidos* with the Garcías, the family who owned the *taller,* had gnawed at him all night long and he dreamed of a life where he could someday have his own place to live and his own money without feeling dependent on someone else's kindness. He had lived here for almost six years. Señor García had found him sleeping in the hay in the attached *caballerisa* the night after his arrival. At first, he had been stern with José and questioned him relentlessly about whose child he was and how he came to be in Cedros. José told him why he had left the orphanage in *ciudad de México*—how the nuns had been brutal, mean, petty, and stingy with food. So constant was his hunger there that the idea of striking out on his own had left him little to fear.

He had made his escape one night with only an extra shirt wrapped around some tidbits of food he was able to steal and hide. He wasn't sure where to go but he had heard others talk about the trains. So, once he was in the streets of the city, he quickly realized he had to act fast, and he sparingly asked for directions to *los patios de trenes*. He had walked most of the night and only a short while before the sun rose, he had found an open cargo car and slipped inside unnoticed by anyone. As the train began to move, it rocked him to sleep and when he woke again, it was once again dark. He had no idea where he was, but he knew he did not want to disembark in a large city because he found it daunting to think of navigating another crowded city with an overwhelming number of strangers.

Afraid to leave the train, for the next few days (was it two or three?) he only allowed himself to peek through cracks in the walls. Most of what he saw was desert. He got off one night in search of food because despite being careful, what little he had brought with him was now reduced to crumbs. Wandering around the trainyard, he found a canvas bag with someone's lunch in it. Snatching it quickly he started to run back to the train. As he turned a corner and crossed a trestle, he saw two men inspecting his boxcar—he thought of it that way now. He had left the door open, and this had drawn their attention! The men walked up and down looking for stowaways until the train left so he had no choice but to watch his ride slowly pull away. He decided he would take his bounty and find a place to sleep and see what opportunities the new day brought him.

The next morning, he wandered around the western outskirts of town and a family came by in a wagon drawn by two horses. The woman spoke to her husband, and they stopped to ask him if he knew if this was the road to Torreón.

"I have no idea," he said, "I'm not from here."

"Where are you from?" the woman asked. He didn't want to say that he had snuck aboard a train several days ago, so he said, "I don't know."

Image 7   Early 20th Century train routes from Mexico City. Rail transport in Mexico. https://en.wikipedia.org/wiki/Rai l_transport_in_ Mexico. Accessed 03/19/20

"Are you from here? Is your family looking for you?" they asked.

He shook his head.

"Where are you going then?"

"I'm not sure. North? Very far," he said.

The couple whispered to each other for a bit and then the man said, "Listen, we are going to a little town outside of Torreón, San Pedro de las Colonias, to go live and work with my brother. You can come with us, if you wish. When we get there, we can find a place in Torreón for you to stay that helps children get new parents."

His first thought was, "No way," but then he figured that a few days of food and shelter would suit him and allow him to ponder his next move. He nodded and hopped aboard. Much later that night they made camp near the small town of Cedros. After a warm meal of dried meat, beans, and tortillas, he was given a thin bedroll not too far from the fire. In the middle of the night, he woke up and remembered where he was and what the nice couple had proposed. He did not want to risk being taken to another orphanage so, as grateful as he was to these kind strangers, he decided to leave and see what he could find in the town. An hour later, after surveying the town, he crept into a corral with horses, fluffed up some hay in the corner and curled up to sleep.

That was about six years ago. At 13, he wasn't sure of his age, José was now bigger, stronger, smarter, and learning to work with his hands. And he was beginning to think about his future. Señor García, *el jefe,* had found him asleep the morning after he first arrived and although he chastised him, he gave him food and said he could stay there if he was willing to clean, do chores, and help him in the shop. He readily agreed. Food, a roof over his head, and someone who could protect him without turning him over to the authorities were more than he had dared dreamed for himself. Over the years, he had met many customers, many of whom were friends with Señor García, and they often spoke of how difficult it was to make a living in such a small pueblo. Weeks ago, he had listened with interest when the men spoke of the Garcías' plans to go *al norte*. They had spoken about how El Presidente Porfirio Díaz's modernization policies benefited only the rich and had made life harder for men who had to work the land for others. It was rumored, Señor García said, that one could get paid by the hour *en los estados unidos* and accumulate enough to feed their family and buy their own land. There were many jobs working in construction or with the rapidly developing railroads in *Tejas*. Señor García had noticed him listening with interest and said, *"¿Qué te parece, Pepe? ¿Quieres ir al norte con nosotros? El Siglo XX ha hecho posible una nueva vida."* He was not his father, but José could not help but look at Señor García for help in answering the question. He shrugged and said, "You are your own person, *hijo,* so the decision is yours, but *you* have to think about your future. Life will be hard here and there is no certainty that whoever buys my business will let you stay here." With that, José did not hesitate and said, *"Sí, quiero ir!"* When he said those words emphatically, José felt like he was taking a blind leap into the unknown, but he also felt like he was taking control over his destiny. Plans had proceeded quickly and the day for departure had arrived. In just a few hours they would begin the journey northward. It had already been decided that he would travel as a family member—as a son.

***

Irineo and Adelaida Olvera: Los Padres de Maria Olvera, circa 1915

In Parras de la Fuente, Irineo Olvera spoke with his wife, Adelaida. It was dark as they sat at a table in the center of the courtyard of their home where they often ate family meals. The year was 1915. Irineo was in his mid-50s now. For over 30 years he had been a *cochero* for the Madero hacienda. It was work that paid him well and garnered him respect from his friends and neighbors. He was now being addressed with the title of Don and in many respects his life was good, but he worried about his five children—all daughters—who, as they matured, had begun to attract the unwanted lascivious attention of soldiers and rebels alike. Life in Parras had been peaceful for most of his life, and he had done particularly well. But when Francisco, the son of Don Francisco and heir apparent of the hacienda, had been elected the President of Mexico and had then been assassinated in 1912 in the capital, life on the hacienda had taken a downturn. Everyone's spirits were deflated.

The Madero hacienda was vast, consisting of ranching, wine making, silver, textiles, and cotton enterprises but everything was tinged with uncertainty now. Added to this was the constant threat of conflict between rebels led by Francisco Villa and President Díaz's army. Villa had immediately risen to the challenge posed by Madero to overthrow Díaz. One of the early battles was in the center of Parras with the military occupying the courthouse. To get the soldiers to abandon the courthouse-turned-garrison, Villa's forces had burned the courthouse down.

Image 8   Irineo Olvera, circa 1915. Mendoza family archives.

Though Villa was successful in rousting the army and the battle moved elsewhere, Irineo and Adelaida had been struck with fear at the proximity of the battle less than a mile from their home. This incident made it clear just how vulnerable the townsfolk were in the midst of an unpredictable war. He remembered that in the aftermath of the battle of Parras, most of the family had to go in and testify to their age, marriage, and baptism dates so official records could be recreated. While Irineo agreed with the need for change and had been excited when the young idealistic Francisco had been elected, he had begun to be disillusioned with the never-ending war. The Maderos were one of the richest families in all of Mexico, and while Irineo felt that there were too many disenfranchised people, he did not think the poor could manage the country as well. Francisco's idealism seemed like it could promote gradual change—but it was not to last and now the country was a powder keg about to explode again.

Ever since the revolution had started five years ago, their sense of safety had felt precarious. Soldiers and rebels alike would come around, especially at night, bang on the door with their guns, get everybody out, and harass them. They were supposedly seeking young men to join their efforts, but the Olvera house was only full of teenage girls. Their eldest daughter, Juana (24), had already married and moved to Texas. Each time these house inspections occurred, Irineo and Adelaida watched the dishonorable way these soldiers leered at the girls, and they feared for the lives of their remaining four daughters: Luisita (Luisa, 20), Quita (Jesusita, 17), Maria (14), and Chonita (Encarnacion, 12).

Under the stars, Irineo and Adelaida huddled, whispered, and devised a plan to keep their daughters safe. This above all was what was important even if it meant sending them away. Lupita, a niece and older cousin of the girls, lived in Beaumont, Texas, where she managed a boarding house for laborers who worked in construction and the surrounding oil fields. Maybe she could be a refuge for the young women as they transitioned into a new society.

***

Zapopan and Felix Martínez, circa 1923, Agujita, Coahuila

Zapopan nodded as Felix, her husband, told her that his mother had called a meeting of the entire family, including spouses. Felix had ten brothers who lived and worked in mines and on farms in nearby towns, Escobedo, Lampazos, Abasolo, Monclova, and Esperanza. While they had survived the turmoil of the revolution, the recent assassination of Pancho Villa at his ranch about 350 miles to the west of them reminded them that the turmoil and violence could rise quickly. In the meanwhile, for more than a decade, there had been no improvement for the lives of everyday people in Coahuila. The ongoing turmoil in the capital exacerbated feelings of unease and they worried that any day now tragedy would hit close to home. Peace and a better quality of life, ideas that had inspired support for the Revolution in its early days, had still not been realized as debates about reform and social change continued to disrupt life throughout the country. Felix and Zapopan had only been married for four years, but they had three daughters, Purificación, Socorro, and Esther who Zapopan desperately wanted to protect as she feared for their safety, growing up in this tense and dangerous time.

Felix and Zapopan had met at a Cinco de Mayo celebration in Agujita just a few years earlier. From this time on, Felix visited Zapopan as often as possible, even though they lived far apart. Finally, about a year later, when Zapopan was 16 and Felix was 17, they were married on August 3, 1919. Felix worked eight hours a day, six days a week and received only two pesos a day. Marrying Felix at such a young age was not something she regretted. As a mechanic's assistant at one of the local mineral mines, he only made a small salary, but it was better than working underground where work was dangerous. Just a year earlier Felix had been burned very badly in a fire. When he had tried to escape, he had climbed under some metal rafters and burned his back badly.

Zapopan's sister, Pepa, had died in that fire. On top of all this, the arrival of the railroad in Coahuila meant that small farmers faced pressure from agribusiness that sought to acquire land and mass produce food for distribution elsewhere. The newlyweds lived in a small rented house until Zapopan's grandmother, Margarita Rendon, invited them to live with her on her small ranch. She taught Zapopan how to be frugal and use her money wisely, so they wanted for nothing. However, Felix's mother and brothers were tired of barely eking out a living and not knowing if they would come out of the mines every time they went underground because the owners were notorious for cutting corners to maximize profits.

There had been talk, whispers mostly, of going north. It was said that work in the *piscas* was plentiful in *Tejas* and that one could start a new life there. Zapopan's family had been in this area for

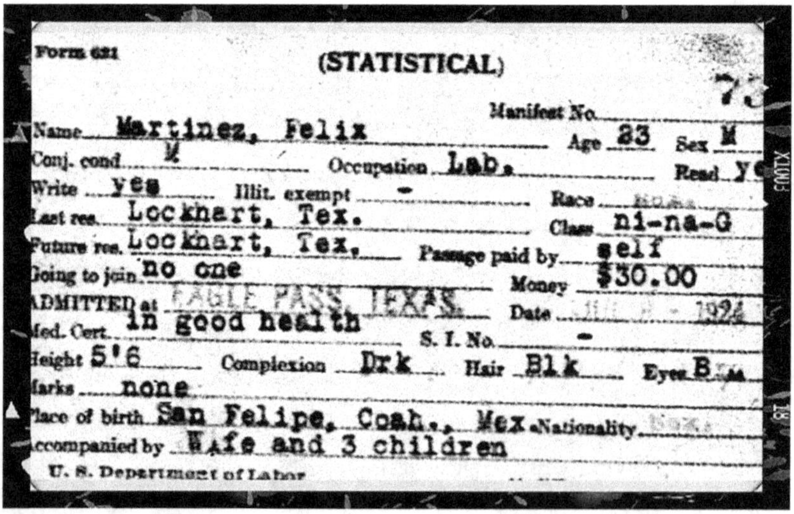

Image 9   Original crossing of the Martinez family via Eagle Pass, TX, July 8, 1924. Accessed via Ancestry.com 09/12/2022.

many, many generations. She could hardly imagine leaving, and yet the prospect of a safer, more peaceful, place to raise their daughters where jobs and food were plentiful was appealing. When the family met, *doña* Maximiana, Felix's mother, confirmed this plan. She had spoken to family who had received word that there were jobs to be had. Maximiana did not want her sons and their family's lives to be at risk. A friend had written about jobs picking cotton in a place called Lockhart, Texas. The plan was to leave in a month, *doña* Maximiana said. "Say your goodbyes, sell your land, take only what is necessary and we will depart on the first of July." They agreed that a week before the proposed date of departure they would gather again to assess their collective finances and determine if they could afford a train; if not they would travel by horse-pulled wagons with the minimum needed to start anew.

The large family parted ways knowing that they would see each other again soon. Each seemed to be thinking solemnly about this decision. Some were worried about the unknown, some were eager to start anew in a place that held great promise, but all were sad to be leaving their homeland and for the circumstances that seemed to make this move inevitable. When they returned to their small home, Zapopan couldn't help but feel a strange mixture of sadness, relief, and anxiety about the unknown. She thought about how she would tell her mama of their plans. She knew her parents had also spoken of going *al norte,* but she also knew that being separated would be hard for both of them. She assumed her mother would be supportive, no matter how sad it made her, and tell her that her husband and his family were making the right decision for the right reasons. She, also, would want her daughter and grandchildren safe. Zapopan wondered if perhaps the time was right for her parents to consider taking their large family north as well.

A time of transition

José arrived in Brownsville, Texas with Señor García and his family circa 1903. He crossed the border claiming the García surname as his own. He was excited for the chance to experience a fresh start in a new place. The Garcías treated him well. He was required to go to school when they arrived in Houston, so they helped him prepare by going over and enhancing the basic reading and math skills he had picked up from other kids in Cedros. Social expectations were such that the law only required him to reach the equivalent of sixth grade. It was understood without being said that he would work and contribute to the García household as children in all working families were expected to do. Work as a laborer did not require much more education than fundamental reading and math so once he could show he knew what sixth graders should know, how to read and write, he no longer went to school.

They lived in Second Ward, a neighborhood that many other new immigrants from Mexico gravitated toward because here one could find others who spoke Spanish as well as street vendors and *tienditas* that sold food that was familiar. By the time José was 16 he was an itinerant assistant to cement masons. In this capacity, he and several other young men were picked up at the corner of Navigation and Lockwood Drive every morning at 7:00 a.m. to be hauled away to construction sites all over the city—usually downtown or in the fancier residential neighborhoods near Rice Village where they created columns for houses and patios, and poured smooth large concrete floors in multiple story buildings.

Early twentieth century Texas

José Mendoza was the first family member of mine to cross the Rio Bravo going north. His future wife, María Olvera, would cross at the beginning of the second decade of the new century, and my maternal grandparents, Felix Martínez and Zapopan García, would make the trip northward with Felix's large family to the cotton fields near Lockhart, Texas in 1924. Though spanning a period of two decades, my family arrived during a sustained period of major economic, cultural, and political change in the region, the country, and the world.

At the turn of the century, Texas was undergoing rapid transition in a number of areas. Fifty-two years after the signing of the Treaty of Guadalupe Hidalgo in which Mexico ceded its northern territories to the United States following the Mexican American War of 1846–1848, and 35 years after the Civil War had divided the USA, Texas exemplified a hybrid of US southern and southwestern cultures. While cattle and cotton had been central to the Texas economy, the agricultural system was undergoing major change which led to a second deterritorialization of Mexicans and *Tejanos* in South Texas. The first instance had occurred in the immediate aftermath of the successful battle for Texas Independence from Mexico in 1836. Not only were great swaths of land given away to entice Anglos to move to Texas, but in the aftermath of the US-Mexican War, the land rights of Mexicans in Texas were not protected as was agreed to in the Treaty of Guadalupe Hidalgo.

Throughout the second half of the nineteenth century, many *Tejanos* lost their land via legal and extralegal means, be it in English-only court battles trying to defend Spanish land grants where, even if they won, they often had to give a significant part of the land to unscrupulous lawyers for their exorbitant legal fees. The anti-Mexican sentiment among Anglos was so pervasive that many newcomers felt they had a right to anything Mexicans had and that they could take it with impunity. Mexican landowners experienced violence wrought upon them by squatters who laid claim to their land by settling there and then resisted any efforts to impede them. Many Mexican American landowners were forced to abandon their land in fear for their lives because they could not count on law enforcement to protect their claims.

Even as Mexican nationals, like my family, fled their home country, Texas was earning a reputation for legal and extralegal violence against Mexicans. Violence in Texas, especially South Texas, in the first two decades of the twentieth century was horrific. It was made worse by the role of the Texas Rangers whose very origins were steeped in a vigilante approach to settling Texas by keeping Anglo settlers safe from Indigenous people and Mexicans. In fact, although they were not officially established until 1835, in 1823 Stephen F. Austin hired ten men to act as "rangers" in order to wage an informal war against the Karankawa tribe in South Texas to facilitate Anglo settlement. They succeeded. The violence wrought by law enforcement officials like the rangers was often cloaked by legal authority and thus sanctioned implicitly. As John Phillip Santos has noted:

> Your opinion of the Texas Rangers likely reflects something about how you or your ancestors first entered

TEXAS FOREVER!!

The usurper of the South has failed in his efforts to enslave the freemen of Texas.

The wives and daughters of Texas will be saved from the brutality of Mexican soldiers.

Now is the time to emigrate to the Garden of America.

A free passage, and all found, is offered at New Orleans to all applicants. Every settler receives a location of

EIGHT HUNDRED ACRES OF LAND.

Image 10   Texas Forever. 1836 Advertisement for land to new settlers in Texas. Briscoe Center for American History. Texas Broadside Collections, file photo 73.93.

into the epic tale of the Lone Star State. If you're the descendant of Anglo settlers who squared off against fierce indigenous resistance and recalcitrant, long-settled Tejanos, then you probably regard the Rangers as the venerable knights-errant of the sprawling Central Plains and southern brush country, the guardians of civil order on the lawless frontier, ever dutiful in their white cowboy hats, ringed silver-star badges, and Colt .45 sidearms. If your forebears were Tejanos whose colonial patrimonies were stolen, often violently, then you may believe the early Rangers to have been nothing more than bloodthirsty thugs for hire, lawless instruments of white supremacy. (Santos, 2020)

The heroic image of the Texas Rangers as agents of the law has been tarnished as numerous historians of the late twentieth and early twenty-first centuries have more closely scrutinized their vigilante role. Historian Monica Muñoz Martinez reminds us that in the campaign to control those seen as outsiders (non-whites), the same trope of a menacing masculinity that was projected onto African Americans was used in depicting Mexican men as a violent and out of control threat to Anglo women, and casting them as foreigners without regard for their citizenship status only advanced their efforts (Muñoz Martinez, 2018). She states that "By 1919, the murder of ethnic Mexicans had become commonplace on the Texas-Mexican border, a violence systematically justified by vigilantes and state authorities alike" (Muñoz Martinez, 2018). Extralegal acts of violence are often overlooked in lynching statistics. The decade from 1910 to 1920 was extraordinarily violent with the numbers of ethnic Mexicans in Texas killed ranging from 300 to several thousand. Just as it did in Northern Mexico, the arrival of the railroad in Texas radically changed the landscape and economy of South Texas and, in doing so, changed people's relationship to the land as workers and owners. Just as Mexican migration northward was ramping up due to the Mexican Civil War, the need for labor in the railroad and farming industries drastically increased. Naveena Sadasivam informs us that by 1920 "Traditional ranching all but ended [in South Texas] and large-scale commercial farming began to take hold" (Sadavism, 2018). The move toward industrial agriculture was hastened with the arrival of the railroad. Land prices increased drastically, and *Tejano* landowners were further deterritorialized by land taxes they could not afford to pay. Simultaneous with this displacement of Tejano landowners was a concerted effort to promote land availability for Anglo outsiders from the Midwest. Advertisements highlighted cheap land, plentiful water, a mild climate, and cheap Mexican labor (Sadavism, 2018). According to Frances Dressman, booster literature in the valley helped shape a race discourse through advertising and imagery that relied on the fusing of Mexican laborers with the landscape, just another natural resource to be exploited. To achieve the desired goal of enticing potential farm owners from outside the region, Mexican workers had to be portrayed as passive, docile, and exploitable (Dressman, 1987, p. 143).

While this strategy may have been idiosyncratic to South Texas, a similar version was used to appeal to potential business investors in Houston as well as to Black and Brown workers as a means of enticing them to move to Houston. In an overview of booster literature for Houston in the late nineteenth and early twentieth centuries, Dressman provides a concise summary of how Houston was promoted as an ideal city that was progressive, healthy, accessible by railroad and sea, with a high-quality infrastructure, replete with high rises, and a plentiful workforce. She notes that:

> Houston was not content being the commercial center of the region. It actively sought the ingredients it needed to transform itself into a major metropolitan area: immigrants, capital, and, most of all, industrial development. Withal, it was not foolish enough to forget that it was still a Southern town replete with a warm climate and a charming style of life.

> The sweet fragrance of the magnolia could be as enticing as the clanking wheels upon the rails or the acrid smell of smokestacks. Booming yet blooming, Houston according to the booster had no minorities, no urban blight, no recessions. It saw itself as a Southern city where refinement was inbred, but with a Northern temperament that thrived on competition. (Dressman, 1987)

Houston thus became an appealing alternative for workers even as Houston's business, civic, and political leaders began to craft Jim/Juan Crow policies that left a clear imprint of southern racism embedded in it.

Interestingly, as intense as racial politics were in Texas, in Hollywood, and thus across much of the nation, the "Latin lover" type was emerging as a hot commodity in the silent era of film. The dark, handsome, lover character in popular films was not exclusively Latino, but many Latin American actors within and outside of the USA achieved success in this era. Actors such as Ramón Navarro, Gilbert Roland, and Emilio "El Indio" Fernández, who served as the model for the Academy Award trophy that later came to be known as the Oscar, achieved great success in the film industry. Alongside them were Latina actresses, such as Lupe Velez, Dolores Del Rio, and a bit later Margarita Carmen Cansino (a.k.a. Rita Hayworth), and actors such as Anthony Quinn. The Latin lover's popularity waned when films with sound emerged in the 1930s. The accents of Latina/o actors were not received well in the Depression era when anyone perceived as a foreigner was cast under suspicion (See *The Bronze Screen: 100 Years of the*

Latino Image in American Cinema [2002] for an excellent analysis of the rise and decline of Latinos in Hollywood).

It is quite possible that my grandparents did not know all the risks they might have faced if they had settled in South Texas. In all likelihood they bypassed South Texas as a possible destination and chose Central and East Texas as the place to start their life in the United States due to readily available jobs and familial connections. This does not mean, however, that they were able to avoid racial animus and harsh working conditions. While animosity against Mexicans may have been particularly strong along the southern border, across the state Anglo Texan assumptions about their superiority shaped local and state culture, politics, and policy in ways that disenfranchised and disadvantaged ethnic Mexicans; this was especially true in locales where Mexicans did not have a long-standing presence, such as East and North Texas.

The Mexican community emerges in Houston

In the early years of the twentieth century, Houston was slowly transforming from a biracial city with an Anglo and African American racial dynamic into a multiethnic, multiracial metropolis. As Tyina Steptoe astutely notes, this dramatic shift was catalyzed by overlapping migrations of African Americans from Louisiana and other parts of the South who were attracted to job opportunities with the railroad and a vibrant African American community (Steptoe, 2016, p. 66). Early in its history, Houston was geographically and politically organized into wards, which went from four to six. By 1905, these wards stopped serving as geopolitical units, but they did become touchstones for different ethnic and cultural communities. For instance, African Americans built a strong infrastructure for Black economic and cultural autonomy as a way to advance self-protection even as leaders of the city enacted Jim Crow laws to buttress segregation and discriminatory practices. While African Americans lived in several areas across the city, the Third and Fifth Wards in particular were densely populated by African Americans. In contrast, the Second Ward became known as the locus of Mexican American residents even as they too were geographically dispersed across the city. In contrast to other cities throughout the southwest, no exclusively Mexican settlements existed at this time. In 1910, there were slightly less than 100 Spanish-surnamed persons living in Houston. About 15 percent of these people worked within the railroad system in one capacity or another. Another 15 percent listed their occupation as laborer. Other identified jobs included waiter, dishwasher, cook, clerk, tailor, and barber. There were also tamale, chili, and candy peddlers (Treviño, 2006).

Simultaneous with the start of the Mexican Revolution in 1910, the oil industry began emerging as a new area for jobs and economic growth. With the arrival of the railroad in the late 1800s, agriculture became a booming industry, but with the rapid growth of the oil industry, agriculture was supplanted by petroleum as Texas's leading industry. A huge supply of cheap labor was needed in the agricultural, oil, construction, railroad, and shipping industries. Mexican immigrants and migrants from other parts of the state began coming to Houston where employment was readily available. According to Zaragoza Vargas, the railroad industry and the Ship Channel were some of the main recruiters of Mexican workers. Oral histories from the era reveal that poor *mexicanos* arrived in Houston looking for work while elite *mexicanos* went to Houston in search of safety for themselves and their family. According to Steptoe, by the late 1920s, "the railroad yards and ship channel docks held the promise of wage labor for farmers and sharecroppers, and thousands responded" (2016).

Around this time, the Second Ward began emerging as a place for the development of an ethnic Mexican enclave. Our Lady of Guadalupe Church on Navigation Boulevard was opened in 1912 to serve the growing Spanish-speaking community (Struthers, 2012). It included a school that taught classes in English and Spanish. Rusk Elementary, which previously catered to children of prominent Anglo families, was slowly transformed into a school that served Mexican children. The Rusk Settlement House increasingly provided social, educational, health, and recreational services for ethnic Mexicans. Arnoldo De León notes that a Mexican presence could be found in several other wards in Houston, though none immediately competed with the Second Ward in size and density. In 1911, Magnolia Park, a previously all-white suburb east of Second Ward, began transforming into a Mexican barrio as work on the Ship Channel began in earnest and new laborers needed housing nearby. Founded as an unincorporated community in 1890, Magnolia Park was seven miles downstream from downtown Houston off Bray's Bayou. Developers had planted almost 4,000 magnolia trees there to attract future residents. Though Anglos first inhabited the town, ethnic Mexicans began arriving by 1911, first settling in the area filled by sand dredged from the turning basin and known as El Arenal, or the Sands. Most of the new settlers worked as laborers, laying railroad tracks or dredging and widening Buffalo Bayou. Others loaded cotton on ships and railroad cars or helped construct the Ship Channel. While Anglo residents tolerated the presence of Mexicans because they were an important source of needed labor, the trustees of the Harrisburg school district in Magnolia Park decided to build a separate school for Spanish speakers in 1920. Immaculate Conception Church was nearby, but Mexicans were not allowed to enter the pews, so they had to remain standing even if seats were available (De León, 1989). Even though Houston was growing rapidly in this era, most Mexican workers were limited to employment as laborers in significantly lower paid jobs where they built sewers, worked on the railroad, or in the fields. A significant amount of the *mexicanos* coming to Houston at this time were refugees and exiles from Mexico who expected to return home one day.

Houston grew rapidly and the growth of this demographic was also steady. De León estimates that the Mexican population grew from 6,000 to 15,000 in 1930. A 1923 report on literacy in Harris County revealed that there were 1,500 foreign-born Mexicans in the county at that time. Between 1920 and 1930, Houston grew 111 percent from 139,000 to 292,000. In the 1920s, the greatest growth of the Mexican community took place in Magnolia Park. In the 1920s, it still had unpaved streets and homes which lacked water, electricity, and gas service. In 1926 it was incorporated into Houston, and it was well on its way to being the largest Mexican barrio. (Kleiner, Magnolia Park, TX, TSHA).

Local residents made a distinction between Second Ward and Magnolia. Many saw the Second Ward as being comprised of Tejanos, internal migrants who were more Americanized than the mostly immigrant population who made up the residents of Magnolia. The culture, political outlook, and experiences of the residents of these barrios were seen as distinctive. In Magnolia, Navigation emerged as the main street of commerce in the barrio. Yet, the city was growing fast and, as is often the case, infrastructure had not kept up with growth and insufficient housing, unpaved roads, and sanitation (outside privies were common) were prevalent (De León, 1989).

Nevertheless, as Magnolia's Mexican population grew, the community began to build an economy oriented toward its working-class residents. Magnolia had its own business district by the 1920s on Navigation Boulevard with Spanish speaking entrepreneurs from the neighborhood (De León, 1989). There was work in refineries, compresses, and other ship channel related businesses. Socially, racial animus against Mexicans was strong. According to De León, "… Jim Crow laws applicable to Black people extended to Mexicans" (De León, 1989). As had occurred in the Second Ward, with the departure of Anglo populations in still emerging barrios of the Second Ward, larger homes were converted into rooming houses. As Mexicans began to dominate Magnolia, Anglo residents moved out and separate schools and churches emerged. On November 8, 1926 at 700 75th Street, Immaculate Heart of Mary Catholic Church was opened and it became the primary church for ethnic Mexicans to attend in Magnolia. Presbyterian and Pentecostal churches followed soon thereafter to serve Magnolia. Rusk Settlement House launched an ambitious Americanizing effort that involved recreation, cooking, and English language classes. Girl Scout and Boy Scout troops were established. While De León notes that it is unclear how effective Rusk Settlement House was, it loomed large as a symbol of Americanization that pervaded US culture at this time. Americanization programs were intended to assist new immigrants adapt to their new society by accelerating their ability to adapt to the dominant social, cultural, and political practices of their adopted country; this included teaching English language skills, citizenship classes, social support, childcare, clothing, and food assistance. Thus, it was that settlement houses, schools, unions, and factories became fertile, if not controversial, sites for assistance and assimilation efforts that "sought to eliminate any visible marker of difference between Americans and immigrants."[1]

Lorenzo De Zavala Elementary School was the first ethnic Mexican majority school in Houston. It had been built because Anglo parents had been worried about the high number of Spanish-speaking students attending the white schools in Magnolia Park. Education policies still stigmatized Spanish speakers, however. For instance, in 1918 the Texas legislature outlawed any language other than English being used for curriculum and instruction, and thus speaking Spanish in the classroom and playground was prohibited for students at De Zavala. These restrictions reinforced notions of Anglo supremacy.

There were two forms of segregation in Houston schools. The most overt form was legally segregated schools for Black students under Jim Crow. The more covert model was the segregation internal to Anglo schools for non-English speakers—it was segregation in practice, but not codified by law. Thus, at the local level "the culture of Jim Crow fostered a racial logic that promoted hierarchies and social differences in language and religious custom" (De León, 1989, p. 97).

A number of self-help and mutual aid organizations emerged to provide support and assistance. In May 1919 in Magnolia, the Sociedad Mutualista Mexicana "Benito Juarez" was established. The *Sociedad* provided assistance for members during times of sickness or death, and it worked for the betterment of the community, promoted linguistic and cultural retention, served as a locus for entertainment and social cohesion. It did not promote Americanization. Presumably oriented to *mexicanos*, these organizations like Mexico Bello were also trying to demonstrate the civility and beauty of Mexican culture to mainstream society to counter the explicit and rampant racism of the time. Sports associations sponsored by Mexican-owned businesses flourished, along with social clubs like the Club Cultural Recreativo Mexico Bello, founded in 1924 (De León, 1989).

Magnolia Park was annexed by the city of Houston in October 1926. By 1929 Magnolia Park, surrounded by refineries, factories, textile mills, industrial plants, and wharves, was the largest Mexican settlement in Houston. The Escuela Mexicana Hidalgo, a private school organized to preserve Mexican culture, was established in the community by 1930. A branch of the League of United Latin American Citizens was organized at Magnolia Park in 1934, and a Ladies LULAC council in 1935. In addition, other political and cultural organizations were activated to provide recreation and promote Mexican American culture, and some of them even actively protested segregation in the city.

Club Feminino Chapultepec was established in the early 1930s. It was organized as a subgroup out of the YWCA on Navigation. Anglo women initially resisted allowing Mexican women to use the facilities and claimed it was because of religion. Early on

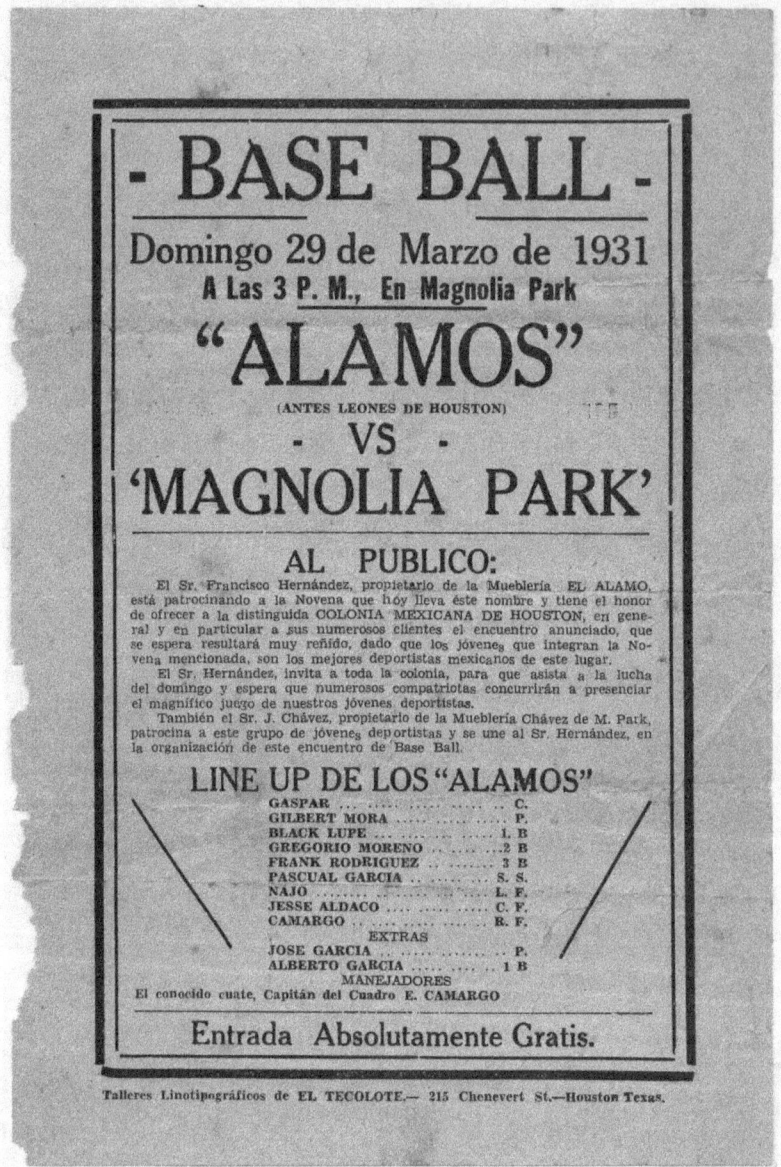

Image 11 El Tecolote. [Advertisement of a baseball game, Alamos versus Magnolia Park], poster, March 21, 1931; Reprint courtesy of Houston Metropolitan Research Center at Houston Public Library.

ethnic Mexican women advocated against discrimination and wrote a "Letter from Chapultepec, a 10-point manifesto critiquing the use of ethnic slurs and the negative portrayal of Mexicans in film" (Kreneck, 2014). They also emphasized their desire to be racially categorized as white. Many others proclaimed pride in their Indigenous heritage even as they advocated for a white classification.

Steptoe notes that around 12,000 Afro-Louisianans and 15,000 ethnic Mexicans lived in Houston by 1930. She states that "…the ethnic Mexican population grew from less than 1 percent in the early twentieth century to over 5 percent in 1940" (2016). Blacks and ethnic Mexicans were an internally diverse group hailing from various parts of the state, nation, and across the southern border. According to Steptoe, Spanish-speaking migrants had a racial subjectivity that "did not conform to the legally enforced Black/white racial binary. Mexicans had their own ideas about race—and these often included a color spectrum that deemed those with dark skin as inferior." Mexicans did not face the same kind of segregation as Blacks as many of them passed for white and were able to participate in white society in ways Blacks could not. Although many sports teams were distinctly ethnic, ethnic Mexicans could participate in baseball leagues, YWCA programs, and although some Jim Crow laws applied to them, they did not have to suffer all the indignities of segregation, such as limitations where they could sit on city buses.

According to Elliot Young, many ethnic Mexicans escaped the trappings of local anti-Mexican Jim Crow (often referred to as Juan Crow) customs as applied to Mexicans if they adopted the "correct" cultural norms, had enough money, married Anglos, or otherwise presented themselves as white. African Americans, understandably, resented this differential treatment which excluded them and allowed some ethnic Mexicans to exercise the same privileges and rights as whites (Young, 2004, cited in Steptoe, 2016, p. 97). "Whatever legal claims to whiteness ethnic Mexicans possessed, segregation was often a matter of local practice—and sometimes depended on the shade of one's skin—rather than official classification," says Steptoe. (2016).

As is demonstrated by the proliferation of groups to serve the Spanish-speaking community in Houston at this time, many ethnic Mexicans sought to preserve their heritage and to use it as a basis for community building even as they resisted being classified other than white and critiqued those who used their light skin to pass as having Anglo or European lineage (Steptoe, 2016).

New destinations

The year is 1920. At 19, María Olvera is a young woman when she arrives via train by way of Piedras Negras/Eagle Pass to Houston with her younger sister Chonita. There they are met by their older cousin Lupita Olvera, who runs a boarding house in Beaumont, about 85 miles east-northeast of Houston. The arrival of María and Encarnación to Beaumont is the culmination of a plan hatched under the stars by Irineo and Adelaida Olvera a few years earlier. Just three short months earlier, their father had died at his home in Parras. Adelaida, the girls' mother was sad to see them go, but also relieved that they would be somewhere far from the instability of Northern Mexico. It was, afterall, a dying wish of Irineo's that they leave and fulfill that plan. Despite promises to return when life was better in Mexico, Adelaida did not expect that her daughters would ever return. They had packed a large trunk of clothes with a few precious pictures and many gifts for Lupita.

The young women traveled by bus to Beaumont. After a few days of acclimating to their new surroundings, Lupita put the girls to work in the boarding house which served men who worked in the oil fields and lumber mills of this small east Texas town which had become the most vivid symbol of the rich potential of Black Gold, the oil industry, in the first year of the twentieth century. Most of the men living at the boarding house were also immigrants from Mexico who appreciated the meals and familiarity of food and the language shared by their countrymen.

Life in Texas was indeed different from life in Parras de la Fuente. Even though Beaumont was a small town, it was located only three miles north of the famous Spindletop oil field that had launched the Texas oil boom. María and Chonita were modest in their dress and in their interactions with the male boarders. In these matters, they followed the advice of Lupita who commanded the respect of the men and regularly reminded those who were married of their obligations to their families. She also established and reinforced house rules that brooked no disrespect to others in the house, especially toward the female staff.

In the summer of 1921, María was introduced to a man ten years her senior who had come to Beaumont to attend a birthday celebration for the husband of a friend of Lupita. Like her, the man was short. He was of dark skin and very quiet, which gave him an air of mysteriousness and gravity. He was very polite and she noticed him looking at her several times from across the yard where the party was held. Eventually, when the food was served and all had sat down to eat, they had their first interaction. He introduced himself as José García. He was very polite and seemed a bit shy. María had become more assertive working in the boarding house and so she kept the conversation going with questions about his family (he had none) and work (he was a cement mason) in Houston. They learned that they were both from Northern Mexico, and that he had been in Texas for quite a bit longer than she. María could tell by the way he looked at her tenderly that he was interested in her. She found him intriguing and when goodbyes were said that evening, he looked her in the eye and said, "I hope to see you again, soon." She looked at him and said, "Yes, me too." José took that reply as a sign that she would not spurn him if he called on her. Thus began a long and slow courtship made all the more challenging by the almost 90 miles between Houston and Beaumont.

José took every occasion available to him to visit, but this was often limited to once, maybe twice, a month. On his first visit following the birthday party he made a point of speaking to Lupita and asking if it was acceptable to visit with María. Often, this meant sitting in the drawing room and talking. Sometimes there was a meal. Only after a few months did he venture an invitation for a walk or a visit to the local ice cream parlor. María would always ask permisison of Lupita before accepting an invitation, and when they left the house, younger sister Chonita often accompanied them as a chaperone. After a few months, he asked María if Chonita might not be interested in meeting a friend of his, Salvador García, with whom he had traveled from Mexico. She agreed and soon there was a double courtship going on and the couples kept each other company, though they allowed just enough space for each couple to develop close relationships with one another.

While José was not an avid talker, he did have a dry sense of humor and an interest in other people that appealed to María. He also proved to be a good listener as she shared stories about the boarders or spoke of how much she missed Parras and her family. She asked many questions about life in Houston and he answered as best as he could. While he had been to see some musicians and folklorico dancers, he most often seemed to enjoy attending baseball games with friends, featuring players from the barrios. He also liked to go to Mexican restaurants and some of the smaller neighborhood *cantinas,* but he did not seem to go to the dance halls much. While María was often full of stories of her immediate and extended families, José rarely said anything about his. Only after almost a year of courtship did he share with her that he had grown up an orphan—he had no parents and no family of which he was aware. This explained a lot to María and she felt intense compassion for the loneliness he must have experienced. She wondered why he had not sought out companionship to build his own family when he was younger.

She ventured to ask him this when they had become emotionally close, and he said that not having parents or a family of his own, he wasn't sure he knew how to be a husband or a father. She realized that it took a lot for him to admit this and she assured him he would probably be really good at it and would treasure the experience even more once he took the risk of building a family. "Moreover," she said, "You won't be going through it alone. Your wife will provide guidance and support." José never forgot this, and a little over two years after they started seeing one another, he asked her to marry him and to be the one to help him build a family. Although José was older than Maria by 11 years, he felt she was wiser and he would look to her when plans were to be made. María did not respond to his proposal right away. She said she needed to get counsel and permission from her mother in Parras before any plans could be made.

That permission was received and on September 17, 1924 at Our Lady of Guadalupe Church in Houston's Second Ward they were married with their friends Pedro Rodriguez and Juana Rosa as witnesses. Their marriage was just four months after her sister Encarnación and Salvador García were married. When they went to church, José told María that his surname was actually Mendoza and not García as he had first told her. She said, well, then tell the priest that name for our marriage certificate. He did. The following June, their first child, Margarita, was born. She was followed by Juan in 1927, José, Jr in 1928, Roberto in 1930, and Jesus in 1935. A son, Manuel, would be stillborn in 1938, and their final child, Adelaida, named after María's mother, would be born in 1943.

After their marriage, José moved the family a few times in order to accept the best-paying jobs and minimize his commute to fast-growing coastal towns that served the oil industry. They moved to Texas City for a year while he worked on a long-term job at one of the refineries. That was followed by a move to La Marque to be near another job site. Eventually, around the time José, Jr was born, they settled into Magnolia Park, further east from downtown Houston than Second Ward where José had initially lived with the Garcías and then with friends from work. The 1930 census showed them to be living at 7822 Avenue E. By the mid-1930s they purchased two small homes on a large corner lot at 7925 Avenue G (which was later renamed Canal Street). It is here where the children grew up and the couple lived the remainder of their lives.

When the financial crisis of 1929 initially hit, the residents of Houston were somewhat cushioned by the centrality of the railroad and shipping economies. Construction work was an important ancillary industry to the railroad and shipyards, so José was able to work, though competition was fierce and anti-Mexican sentiment rose sharply among laborers who saw Spanish speakers as an economic threat, a convenient scapegoat for the country's financial woes, and as foreigners who represented a danger to the country's economic and social well-being. These sentiments thrived without regard for the targets' actual citizenship status and many US citizens were also targeted. This was especially true when the workflow was slowed down due to a lack of market demand and the limited flow of cash, and laborers were hit hard by work stoppages and supply chain issues.

By and large, María managed and supervised the household. Depsite her and José only having an elementary school education, they managed to maintain a modestly comfortable lifestyle even if they were a bit crowded in a four-room shotgun house. They grew corn, pears, peaches, and figs on their lot to supplement their diet. Rent from the even smaller house next door helped underwrite their mortgage. During the evenings and weekends, José used his skills with cement to make decorative concrete planters, often in the shape of animals, that were embellished with glass and tiles to bring in extra money. As the boys grew, they pitched in by shining shoes, selling newspapers, and doing odd jobs to earn a few coins, most of which they dutifully handed over to their mother. José Jr often recounted a story of a time during the Depression when his father was sent to the store to buy some medicine. A fierce rainstorm developed while he was gone and he came home without groceries because the dollar bill had flown out of his hands. His mother immediately gave her husband a reproving look and sent him out to look for the money, but he was unable to find it. José Jr says that the next morning he went looking for it paying special attention to the side of the street to which the wind would have blown debris. After an hour of looking he found it against a chain-link fence and happily turned it over to his mom so they could get the groceries that they needed.

The 1940 US Census shows that the Mendozas lived at 7925 Canal St. and paid $12.00/month rent. José's occupation was listed as a cementer who worked for various paving contractors and earned an income of approximately $480 per year. María and José saw that blue-collar workers were especially vulnerable to the economy. This motivated them to encourage their children to get an education but having only an elementary school education themselves, they did not demand educational success of their children.

In some ways, this attitude extended toward their religious practices. María had been raised in a devout family who attended church regularly and who celebrated holy days with reverence. José had no such structure and though he sometimes visited churches out of curiosity, he was not a regular churchgoer until he

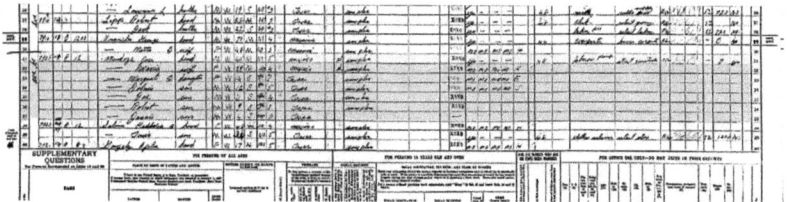

Image 12   1940 U.S. Census. Mendoza family. Retrieved from Ancestry.com on 08/22/2022.

was married. While Margarita enjoyed dressing up and attending church, of her brothers, José Jr was the only one who took a genuine interest in the joyful, glorious, sorrowful, and luminous spirituality of the Catholic church. Not only did he faithfully attend church every Sunday with his mother, he often went on weekdays before school. His devotion was intense and solemn. He often wished he could serve as an altar boy at Immaculate Heart of Mary, a church opened in the 1920s in Magnolia to exclusively serve the Mexican population, but when he inquired the Anglo priest had given him an odd look and said he was not allowed to be an altar boy. Though the priest did not make clear why this was so, José felt it was something about his very being, his kind, that disallowed this, so he accepted the priest's judgment even as he suspected the reasoning was unholy.

Like many children of immigrants, the Mendoza kids served as translators for their parents when interactions with public officials, schools, or doctors called for it. Some of them embraced their parents' vision for them to succeed in school; others sought success in the workforce. In the early 1940s with the war raging in Europe, José Sr, and later his sons, registered for the draft. The boys saw being drafted when they came of age as inevitable and they decided to volunteer. By this time, their names had long ago been anglicized. John joined the navy, Joe the army, and Robert the air force. Eventually, though he was younger, Jesse also joined the army. Margaret's boyfriend and future husband, Robert Gonzalez, lost the bottom half of his leg when he participated in the storming of Normandy Beach on D-day in June 1944.

José and María Mendoza were to live in the United States from the early part of the twentieth century until their deaths in 1974 and 1983, respectively. Although they sent their children to school and aspired for them to be successful in an English dominant society, they never became fluent in English and thus communication with their grandchildren was minimal. They accepted their transition to the USA stoically even as their children became assimilated to varying degrees. Maria did take her chidren to visit family in Parras a few times. Notably, a 1944 border crossing card shows that all four boys traveled with her as they returned from Mexico via Laredo. Her old family home had been gifted to relatives when her mother died in 1922.

This once young couple uprooted from their home by the turmoil of the early twentieth century, succeeded in building a new life in the United States. They witnessed a vast amount of social and technological change, and their lives, their labor, their story is an integral part of the fabric of Houston's history, just as is the thread of so many other lives. They were not rich, but they were safe. According to my father, though he often wished for a more diverse diet, they were never hungry. The beautiful mahogany woodframes that encase my great-grandfather's and my grandmother's photos, and the mere fact that these professionally taken photos from this time exist, suggest that they had the resources to indulge in these luxuries when many others did not. Moreover, because Lupita played a big role in helping my grandmother transition to live in the USA, María remained loyal to her and paid visits to her in Beaumont at least twice a month. And this is one of the reasons that, unlike many others, José and María owned a car when few working-class *mexicanos* did. My grandfather was very proud of this and he only stopped driving when he wrecked the car at a very advanced age with my brother Bobby in it.

I have vivid memories of my grandparents' deaths. José Mendoza, Sr died in May 1974 at the age of 82 of congestive heart failure, and María Olvera Mendoza died in 1983 at the age of 82. My father was their primary caretaker and one reason I recall my grandfather's death was that my father visited him every day he was in the hospital and he deeply impressed me with how tender and caring he was as he spoke to him, tried to make him comfortable, and changed his bedpan and helped him urinate as needed. In those occasions he would ask me to help roll him on his side and my father would gently hold his penis as he relieved himself. My grandmother's last two years were spent at a nursing home off Interstate 10, where my father visited her almost daily.

From the fields to the big city

Border crossing cards reveal that Felix Martinez, Zapopan, and their three young girls crossed the border from Piedras Negras into Texas in January 1923. Records also indicate that his mother and most, if not all, of his brothers and families did so as well. They went directly to Lockhart where they had made a commitment to work the cotton fields. Zapopan's parents and some, but not all, of her siblings, joined them in Texas a year later. For the next ten years Felix and Zapopan would work the migrant trail working mostly in the cotton fields of Central Texas, chiefly Caldwell County, but they also picked vegetables such as corn and okra. In the offseason they began gravitating toward Houston, which had a growing *mexicano* community and where men could find short-term work as laborers to hold them over until the next crop came in. They pitched in and bought a flatbed with stake sides to get them and other workers (for a modest fee to help pay for fuel) to the fields. Picking cotton was backbreaking work made all the more difficult by the glaring heat of Central Texas. The lodging that migrant workers were given was often second or third class—often nothing more than rickety shacks with dirt floors. One was paid by the pound, so picking often necessitated that the older kids and their mothers also worked, though some remained behind to care for the younger children, wash clothes, tend animals, and prepare meals for the family. The Martinezes were fortunate to find employment on a cotton farm that provided them with a large house set aside for migrant workers. They arranged to return to this farm each year for as long as they continued to pick cotton so the families could stay together.

As Felix and Zapopan's family grew, they began to desire more stable work and housing, a life that did not require them to move every year and go through periods of unemployment and no pay. The drought of 1926 was particularly hard as many crops suffered and little work was to be had. In Houston, they experienced firsthand the growing community in Houston's East End. Houston now had two Catholic churches for the Spanish-speaking community. There was even a new elementary school exclusively for Mexicans! They initially lived in the Second Ward

Image 13 Mexican Cotton workers in fields near Corpus Christi, Texas circa 1930s. Hollem, Howard R., photographer United States. Office of War Information.

area of Houston; that's where Geneva was born in their home in 1926. In 1927, the young family moved to Magnolia Park where Mary was born in December of that year.

Although she had only finished elementary school herself, Zapopan wanted her children to have the chance for an education and work that wasn't so hard. By 1931, with the birth of José Philip, their only son, in Caldwell, Texas, Felix and Zapopan's family had grown from the three girls they had upon arrival to seven. Their daughter Dora had also been born in Lockhart in 1929. By 1931, the oldest girls, born in Mexico, were already 11, 9, and 7, and life on the migrant trail was especially hard for them as they moved from school to school. Although a profound intimacy developed among those families that worked and traveled together, schooling became of secondary importance compared to the harsh demands of migrant life.

After the 1931 cotton harvest, Felix and Zapopan rented an apartment in Magnolia near Ave L. It was bittersweet. They were excited about establishing roots, but now the extended Martinez family seemed to be going down two distinct paths, those who continued to work the fields and those who would now make Houston their home. In 1932, Zapopan's parents, Luis and Emeteria, would return to Coahuila. They, too, had migrated northward in the early '20s and it had never been Luis's intention to stay. As he aged, he had often told his boys, "If I die here, take me back to Mexico as quickly as you can and bury me in Escobedo. If you cannot take me right away, burn my body and take my ashes back to where they belong!"

Life in Magnolia was good for the Martínez family. Their family grew until there were nine children, with eight girls and one boy. Aurora, also called Nena, was born in 1933, and Gloria was born in 1941. The kids attended Lorenzo de Zavala Elementary School in Magnolia, and then Deady Middle School on Broadway or Thomas Edison on Avenue I. Not all of them went on to high school, but those who did attended Milby High School. Three of the nine would eventually earn college degrees. With nine children, Zapopan was kept quite busy. She got up every morning to make fresh flour tortillas for the day. My mother recalled that when her father took tacos to work, the men at work wanted to buy them.

Living in Magnolia, Zapopan never had to learn English because she could shop, go to church, and for the most part communicate all in Spanish. She did take English classes at Rusk Settlement and they offered daycare for the children, but her attendance was irregular because there were so many demands on her time. Zapopan was frugal and the younger children wore hand-me-down clothes from their older sisters. As her daughters began to come of age, she supported them working outside the home and socializing at activities sponsored within the neighborhood. The oldest, Pura, was involved with Mexico Bello and aspired to be a socialite above her socioeconomic background.

Work during the Great Depression was infrequent and there were times when the rent was due when the family would keep the curtains closed and lay low if they could not afford to pay the landlord. As was true in the Mendoza household, the wife managed the household finances. Felix was by and large a mellow and happy-go-lucky man who paid the utmost attention to his family, but there are family tales that suggest from time to time he would return home late on a payday with a portion of his check gone because he had stopped to drink a few beers with friends on the way home. Zapopan had little tolerance for this because the margin of error in the household budget was slim. On these occasions she would make him sleep on the porch or go to work the next day without lunch. When his daughters tried to give him food to take to work, they faced their mother's ire. Unlike the Mendoza family, Felix and Zapopan never owned a car. The 1940 census revealed that Pura and Socorro, then young women of 20 and 18, worked as a "saleslady" and "cashier" respectively, selling gas, dry goods, and groceries (1940 US Census). Felix worked as a truck driver at a cotton compress and received $684.00 a year in that capacity. They paid $12.50 a month rent on their house at 7531 Canal St. As was customary in their family, working children gave over their paychecks to their parents to support the household and were given back a portion of their check to use at their discretion.

Zapopan, sometimes called "Popa" by family, was a joyful person who loved to dance and sing songs. To poke fun at herself, she would call herself *sopa de pan* (bread soup). While it took them many years to get a radio, when they did get one, it was tuned to a local Spanish station and was on constantly. She loved to teach rhymes and *dichos* to her children, many of which were passed down to her children through the generations. Her favorite *dicho* was: *Dime con quien andas, y te dire quién eres*. Zapopan was good at making up rhymes to make her children laugh. For instance, when her kids sang the classic English folk song, "Pop goes the Weasel," she would respond by singing *Papas con chorizo*. She was quick and witty as well. When one of my aunts told her mom that she had made some sweets and had intended to share them with her but that she and the kids had eaten them, Zapopan quipped an old proverb, *Sus dientes esta mas cerca que sus parientes*. One of my aunts said that when she would go to stay overnight with her mom in her later years when she was confined to a bed they "… would sing and sing every Spanish song we knew until we fell fast asleep. She loved to sing so much."

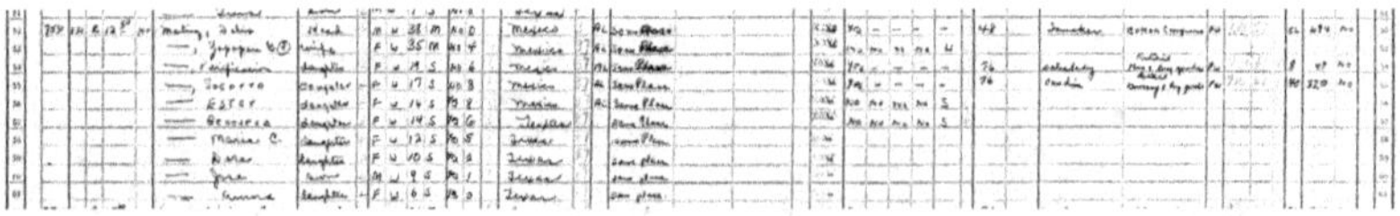

Image 14 1950 U.S. Census. Martinez Family, Retrieved from Ancestry.com on 08/21/2022.

Zapopan was the disciplinarian in the family. In spite of having only a fourth-grade education, she was very handy and could take things apart to fix items in the house, such as her iron. To save money and bring in some extra income, she sewed clothes for her children and made dresses for neighbors upon request. Zapopan insisted that the entire family attend church every Sunday. What she was unable to give her children with money, she provided in other ways. She also raised chickens in the backyard for their eggs and to cook for as many years as she could chase them. Zapopan was a devoted churchgoer and many of her daughters followed her example. They became more involved in church activities as a family when Immaculate Heart of Mary was opened. Christmas was one of the biggest celebrations, and each year after the family attended midnight mass, a *tamalada* was held at the Martinez house. The *tamalada* included tamales, hot chocolate, and sweet bread; after this the presents were opened. Being very poor they could not afford presents, so each year their mother wrote to Goodfellows for presents for the children. The Rusk Settlement House would pass out bread with syrup for holiday treats and the family gratefully incorporated this treat into their celebratory gathering. Despite Zapopan's strong Catholic faith, when Dora, one of their daughters, ran away to a convent in her late teens, Zapopan was devastated. Dora's closest sister, Mary, supported her decision and kept secret her sister's plans to leave so her parents would not thwart Dora's departure.

When able, the Martinezes contributed to the weekly kermesses which raised funds for the church but also provided regular events for neighborhood families to gather. The Salon Benito Juarez was down the street and Zapopan would contribute food for their

Ben giving a tour of the capitol to a group of Senior Citizens from Magnolia. They were brought to the capitol by Fred Tudon (far right) director of H.C.C.A.A. Area 9.

Image 15   Zapopan, center of picture at tour of state capitol with Councilman Ben Reyes. Mendoza family archives. Original source unknown.

meetings and fundraisers as well as help community members in times of dire need. She did this even when times were hard because her sense of responsibility to others grounded her moral compass. She liked to maintain strong ties to her heritage and since her father-in-law had returned home, other than the biannual trips to visit her family in Escobedo, she felt it important to maintain connection to her Mexican heritage.

Felix continued to work in the cotton industry while in Houston, though in a different capacity. The 1940 census listed his occupation as a cotton compress truck driver. In 1950, his occupation was listed as a "Checker" at a cotton warehouse. However, in a question that asked if this person worked in the past week, Felix had not, so his employment may have been erratic or seasonal. As a checker he would have weighed, measured, and checked materials coming into and leaving the warehouse. In the early '40s, Felix and Zapopan had saved enough money to buy a house at 7706 Canal St. In this two-bedroom house they would raise their nine children. Eventually, in the early 1940s, Felix found work as a longshoreman at the Ship Channel, which was very nearby. During the war years, many young men from the area joined the military and labor was scarce, so older and younger than average men could find employment at the shipyard where all work during this time was considered part of one's patriotic duty.

While he worked, but more earnestly when he retired, Felix would gather and crush aluminum cans and collect old newspapers and then take them to be redeemed for cash. My Aunt Geneva recalled taking her grandson, Brian, to visit his great-grandparents; he would go to the garage and help grandpa crush those cans. Grandpa would say *"pura feria, pura feria"* (pure cash, pure cash) and Brian would repeat the words in broken Spanish. She also recalls asking her father how he liked mama's cooking, he would smile and say "not even the president eats as well as I do."

My Aunt Gloria recalls that she spent many years alone with them.

> I was the last one left with them from age 13. I was the only kid there until I was 22. They were wonderful parents. Dad was stricter with my older siblings. By the time I was a teenager he was more understanding, although he still would wait for me on the porch until I returned home from a dance or a date. When I got married, dad's neck and shoulders stooped down and he had to go for treatment.
> My Aunt Tonia came for the wedding, she stayed with my mom to divert attention from my being gone from the house. She made sacrifices. If I wanted to go to dances, she would go with me to Pan American nightclub at night and sit there at a table, and then we would both get on the bus to get home. She did it for

me because she knew I needed the entertainment (I was a teenager). They gave me a *quinceñera*. None of my sisters got one, but I was the youngest. They were very high on education, and always encouraged us.

When her children had almost all left home, Zapopan began raising foster kids. In all, she fostered six children after her own nine had left home. Some were fostered through Catholic charities, others through the Harris County probation department. Many years later they invited Zapopan to their weddings. This was a practice that several of her daughters copied alongside raising their own children; one of her daughters formally adopted a foster child into her family.

Zapopan and Felix loved having visits from their children and grandchildren. They would regularly invite family over on holidays and it was not uncommon to visit them on Sunday and have two or three other families also visiting. In the heyday of their children raising their children in the '70s, the family would rent out a church hall that could hold a party for 100 people. Games would be held, and the climax was a visit from Santa Claus, usually played by one of the uncles.

Sometime in the mid-1990s, Joe Martinez, his wife Lily Martinez, and sister Patricia Martinez, sat with Zapopan at her dining room table and recorded a conversation about her and Felix's journey to the United States from Northern Mexico. Details from that conversation inform this chapter. Zapopan framed the discussion with a poem she had learned in grade school. To honor the importance of this poem to her, I include that poem below as well as a poem I wrote, "Zapopan" in 1998 immediately following her funeral:[ii]

Amor Filial

She is my mother, my treasure,
        I adore her.
I will love her all my life
        without measure.

Did she not stand next to my cradle,
        like no other?
Not just anyone cared for me as a child,
        this is true.

She taught me to walk
        and to talk
How much patience, mother? How much?
        You are a saint.

You are my sweet support.
        So valuable.
By your side, my mother,
        nothing will faze me.

Beside you nothing is a heavy load.
        I fear nothing if I see you.

I believe in you.
Your affectionate, loving words
are divine inflections, sweet sounds.
        I will work for you eagerly and carefully.

And until death comes

> *I want to see you,*
> *Oh, my mother, my treasure.*
> *I adore you.*

Zapopan (1998)

Zapopan . . .
        Was not the name by which I knew her.

Only upon her passing did I first hear
        This name that sounds like a dusty village.
Only then did I realize how little of her I knew,
        Yet she was my abuelita, my grandma Martinez,
… mostly just plain old grandma.

"She was our refuge," I thought
        when I sought to capture shared memories
that could serve as a touchstone for her brood,
        and as I gave a departing eulogy upon the altar, her large heart and soft hands,
        warm in winter and cool in summer,
came to mind as gifts of the everyday sort.

At 94 she was the last of the abuelos to go …
        doing so with full awareness
of her matriarchal role.
        When last I saw her at Xmas '97, she bade me kneel

before her so she could impart a blessing.
       I obeyed with the realization that this
was her despedida,
one she spoke with force, not fear.

3 weeks later, work begun,
       Word of her home demise came
through the phone line.
She stayed long enough for one last Sunday
visit from
       a three-generation line of children.

At three I hid within the folds of her thin
house dress
       when my parents came to retrieve me
after a post-stillborn birth retreat.
       Not understanding, I thought I'd been
left behind for good.
Quickly had I become comfortable with her sweet
smelling and whisper-quiet
       world of a house ensconced by banana
and magnolia trees.

Outside in the leaning garage, I followed
grandpa as he
       pounded aluminum cans and bound
newspapers
for spare change.
       Inside, she moved about her small
kitchen that once fed eleven mouths daily.
Stove, fridge, and sink lined up for easy

maneuvering,
        a table or two that she could turn to
without making her chanclas
go flip
        or flop.

I am told that as a pre-school child I was bilingual.
        I don't remember exchanging many words with her,
but we never had trouble communicating.
        Not even when I was older and my Spanish was broken,
nor later when I struggled to reclaim it and share it with her.
        Her patient eyes listened through my fragmented language.

Once, months after grandpa passed,
        and the dutiful daughters stayed with her nightly to quell her loneliness
I was there when mom could not take her turn
        because she was sick.
After dinner and TV, grandma went to bed.
        Hours later, I heard her wail from behind the closed bedroom door.
"Felix! Felix! Donde estas?" she cried.
        10 minutes of relentless sobbing later,
I gathered the courage to knock on her door,
        afraid to disrespect her grief, afraid to
not reach out.

Minutes passed.

Finally, she peeked out and looked at me with tear-filled eyes.
  "Are you ok, grandma?"
"Si, mi'jo, era una pesadilla, no mas."
  "Okay, I'm sorry grandma," I said.
while trying to say more with my eyes.

Standing before her clan, I said:
  "She was our matriarch, our gran jefita—
the one who
brought us into the world;
  She was the thread that binds us together
into a tight weave of laughter and song.
  And for that I am sure that we are all grateful.
She made it possible for us to be here.
  It is a debt that will take a lifetime
to repay,
but one which we should happily assume
  as we reconcile ourselves with her
absence and move on."

I ponder the totality of her life.
  Zapopan was Mexico to me.
She had an awesome courage, vision, and faith
  to make the journey here … and stayed
when parents and siblings returned to Mexico.
  She was my strongest link to a rich

cultural heritage,
representing strength and perseverance.
    As grandson, I am heir to a legacy that
must be remembered.

I know she had no easy life.
    I know there are many, many things
about her
of which I am ignorant, but
    I know she wouldn't have become the
matriarch she came to be
if she wasn't strong, resourceful, and good.

If there is anything
    I have inherited through the
generations, it is
the living example of our ancestors,
    a sense of responsibility for
and goodness to my fellow human beings.
    I have learned that their hardships have
meaning *in* us.
From grandma, I learned generosity of spirit,
patience, compassion for others,
    and the wisdom of our common past.

No books, tablets, or fancy pen had she, but
    Her knowledge was unsurpassed.
She told me mother, and my mother told me:
    *Dime con quién andas, ye te diré
quién eres.*

I try to honor her life today...
    by the way I live,
by keeping good company,
    by keeping her spirit alive through
rituals of remembrance like this.

Thus she is with me ...
    para siempre.

A friendship is forged (circa 1942)

Just a few blocks from their home on Canal, at Immaculate Heart of Mary Church on 75th at Avenue K in Magnolia, Zapopan and her daughters, Dora and Mary, would often attend early morning mass on weekdays. There they would frequently see a well-dressed, well-coiffed, handsome, young boy attending mass with his mother or by himself. He was about Mary's age, and he, too, lived on Canal just two blocks down the street from them. He would always acknowledge them with a nod of his head, a *buenos días,* and a hint of a smile. Once she noticed him, Mary came to realize that he was a grade below her at Deady Middle School. Soon, they were exchanging hellos and small waves. When they saw each other walking home from school, they often let him walk with them.

And thus, though no one realized at the time, from these small seedlings of kindness, innocent smiles, and polite exchanges, grew a friendship between my parents that would later blossom into a lifelong relationship that would span eight decades.

2
Becoming Americans: surviving, negotiating, and thriving under acculturation

In the first three decades of the twentieth century approximately one million Mexicans migrated to the United States for better jobs and for refuge from the Mexican Revolution. However, the Wall Street Crash in October 1929 slowed down this migration to the United States significantly. Across the country, including in the southwest where many had been born, ethnic Mexicans were often viewed as outsiders despite their nationality or legal status. In this way they became convenient scapegoats for the country's economic woes and were cast as an economic and social threat. Their experience in Houston was no different. According to Jesús Esparza (2011), City of Houston officials accused ethnic Mexicans of being economically harmful and launched raids into their communities.

In 1930, Houston was the twenty-sixth largest city in the country with a little over 293,000 residents. Of these, about 15,000 were of Mexican descent. This was compared to 8,339 first- and second-generation Eastern and Southern European immigrants in Houston at this time. At about 2 percent of the population, and not considered fully white or Black, the ethnic Mexican population was just beginning to emerge as the third significant population group according to Treviño (2006).

Many of the mutual aid societies that aided newcomers modified their assistance to community members to address the economic crisis and rising anti-Mexican sentiment experienced by the community. In the early 1930s, the focus of support for immigrants shifted to supporting the civil rights of residents as it became clear that despite extensive efforts to deport Mexicans, the vast majority of the population was here to stay. An intensive effort to eliminate ethnic Mexicans' use of relief funds from the federal government resulted in a huge number of forced and voluntary deportations of members of this community. A significant number of ethnic Mexicans were forcibly removed despite their legal status as citizens of the United States. Historians surmise that 2,000 Mexicans or approximately 15 percent of Houston's Mexican population in 1930, left in the early years of the Depression. Regular trips to the border were scheduled to depart from the Rusk Settlement House. These trips included those returning voluntarily as well as those who had received deportation orders. In 1931, raids of jobsites netted 152 deportations from the city (De León, 1989). Texas's Mexican-born population was reduced by a third during this time. In all, while estimates vary, between 400,000 and 1,000,000 people of

Mexican descent returned to Mexico from the USA during the Great Depression.

Mexican Americans thus walked a thin line between social inclusion and complete exclusion. In the first half of the twentieth century, when schools were legally segregated by race via Jim Crow laws, Mexican Americans attended schools legally designated for white students. In fact, until 1970 the Houston Independent School District (HISD) counted Latino students as "white" (Kellar, 1996). This did not equate to a better, more inclusive education for people of Mexican descent as they experienced internal segregation in schools or assignment to less well-resourced schools, the trauma of being punished or humiliated for speaking their first language of Spanish in school, disparaging representations of their community in school curricula, and hostile and pervasive anti-Mexican racism. As has been mentioned previously, the first school in Houston with a majority ethnic Mexican student body was Lorenzo de Zavala Elementary School in Magnolia Park. School district administrators had established De Zavala Elementary to alleviate the fears of Anglo parents who were concerned about an increase in Mexican students in area schools.

There was continuity and change during the 1930 to 1945 period. Some immigrants began to shift their outlook and orientation toward the USA being their homeland, while others retained loyalty and orientation toward Mexico. Certainly, pervasive anti-Mexican racism did not help acculturation and acceptance. Continuous arrival of new immigrants reinforced Mexican identity. Cultural affirmation and continuity were supported by Spanish language newspapers, films, community clubs, and organizations. Spanish language newspapers serving Houston's Mexican community included, *El Gaceta, El Tecolote,* and *El Puerto: Seminario Independente de Magnolia Park,* with about 75 percent of the content focusing on Mexico (De León, 1989, pp. 60–62). Numerous musical groups arose, with the most popular being La Orquesta Tipica de Magnolia. The popular singer Lydia Mendoza was born in the Heights neighborhood of Houston in 1916. When she and her family were being repatriated, they stopped in Houston and played to large crowds. Neither ideologically nor politically homogeneous, some elements of Houston's ethnic Mexican community consciously cultivated their Mexicanness even as other segments of the community adapted to their new situation and began identifying ways to actively build a community grounded in their present and future as part of the United States.

In the 1930s, a number of important organizations and social and recreative clubs emerged out of Magnolia to meet the needs of Houston's Mexican descent population. Mexico Bello continued to be popular. Many were for special purposes or met the needs of residents of a particular barrio. Leaders of some of these clubs had underlying motives beyond cultural preservation and assisting members. Some sought to advance the perception of the ethnic Mexican community by demonstrating their decorum and civility upon the dominant community. Funds were raised to assist children within the community. Some of these clubs, such as Club Recreativo Internacional, extended their membership to other Latin Americans. Club Recreatvio Anahuac, Club Recreative Xochimilco, Club Terpoiscore, El Circulo Cultural Mexicano, and Los Amigo Glee Club provided other options for community members to interact with one another (De León, 1989). Alongside these clubs, a number of self-help groups arose. Camp Laurel #2233, El Campamento Navidad 3968 W.O.W., Sociedad Mutualistas Obrera Mexicana, and the Sociedad Union Fraternal were some of the better known ones catering to workers that provided assistance to those in crisis (De León, 1989, p. 69). During the Depression, Immaculate Heart of Mary was expanded to include a nun's convent and the "church grounds became the setting of Kermesses, jamaicas, and noches mexicanas…" It also hosted fiestas patrias sometimes.

The 1930s census showed that about 60 percent of Mexicans in Texas were native born. During this time, a generation of children of immigrants were growing up who saw themselves as US citizens and Tejanos. Simultaneous with the emergence of these organizations were ones that focused on the needs of the Mexican-descent population who had long resided in Texas. (De León, 1989) Some cultural organizations extended their activities to include activities or actions advocating for social equality. Magnolia Park Post 472 of the American Legion was chartered in 1928. Founded in Corpus Christi in 1929, the League of United Latin American Citizens, arose to challenge discriminatory public policies and practices. LULAC Council #60 was established in 1934 in Magnolia Park. They were an advocacy organization that advocated for a more inclusive society through reform not radical change. One organization that arose in 1938 with advocacy as its primary purpose was the Confederación de Organzaciones Mexicanos y Latino Americanos (COMLA). This organization sought to advocate for citizens and non-citizens alike. In many respects, COMLA competed with LULAC by being more inclusive in its approach that extended support for non-citizens. Building a broad-based unity was not easy due to the dispersal of Mexicans in Houston. In 1935 the Latin American Club (LAC) of Harris County was formed. The official language of the club was English. LAC and LULAC #60 coexisted but with LAC being much more active (De León, 1989, p. 86). It organized around education, better parks, youth programming, and advocated for better pay and working conditions as well as public health issues. Notwithstanding its pro-American stance, members faced racial hostility. Despite being more active, LAC united with LULAC in 1939 to be part of the national LULAC. As LULAC grew in size and visibility, its efforts aligned with attempts at Americanization even though it both advocated for ethnic Mexicans and simultaneously left formal and informal racist policies and practices toward other groups unchallenged.

The Depression intensified social hostilities in the workforce and society at large. Jim Crow signs emerged proclaiming the second-class status of Mexican residents. They read: "No Mexicans Hired," "No Mexicans Need Apply," "No Mexicans, for White Only," and "No Chili, Mexicans Keep Out." The Houston City Council adopted an ordinance that required the Port of Houston to guarantee that at least 50 percent of jobs went to whites (De León, 1989).

It was in this climate of harsh anti-Mexican sentiment that my parents were born into and came of age. Hand in hand with this was a persistent drive toward Americanization supported by school, the YWCA, and area settlement houses that encouraged immigrants to leave one's culture, native language, and sentiment toward one's country of origin behind. The intent was to advance assimilation and create "good" citizens by cultivating English language skills, personal hygiene, sanitation, industrial safety and productivity, patriotism and loyalty, and knowledge of American civics education of promoting patriotism and productivity.

María Concepción Martinez[i]

In a small apartment in the front part of a house her parents rented at 7631 Avenue L in Magnolia Park, Maria Concepción Martínez was born on December 8, 1927. She was the fifth child born to Felix and Zapopan. The growing family then consisted of five girls and their parents (Pura, Socorro, Esther, Geneva, and now María). Geneva had been the first one born in Houston as the family had spent its first few years in Lockhart working the fields of a cotton farm. There, the family shared a large field worker house with many of their cousins who had also migrated from Coahuila. In 1925, a Central Texas drought ruined the crops and Felix moved the family to Houston to eke out a living as a contract laborer.[ii] The family would continue to work the cotton fields of Central Texas until 1934 and spent some winters in Houston where other family members resided. Mary's sister Dora was born in 1929 and her brother José in 1931, in Lockhart and Caldwell, respectively. For many years the children looked back with fond memories of life on the cotton *ranchito* where they cohabitated with cousins and played with farm animals. In 1934, however, Zapopan persuaded Felix that they should settle in Houston so the children could get a better education and be exposed to a life that was more financially stable and predictable.

By the time school started in the fall of 1935, Mary, Geneva, and Dora went to the still relatively new school for Mexican children, Lorenzo de Zavala Elementary School. Her older sisters, Pura and

Socorro, went to Milby High School but soon quit for jobs at local stores that would help supplement the family income. Attending school in Houston was hard for the Martinez girls as they had limited exposure to English. Like most children, they listened carefully and quickly started picking up bits of the language here and there from classmates. Classmates who had successfully learned English also helped them understand English words and phrases. They soon learned, however, that they were forbidden to speak Spanish at school, and doing so resulted in punishment. In the third grade Mary switched schools and started going to Immaculate Heart of Mary school. While the nuns were kinder than the teachers at De Zavala, the students were still not allowed to speak Spanish. Mary was very self-conscious about her limited English vocabulary and Spanish accent, so she remained quiet in school. Although she loved reading and math, she rarely volunteered to answer questions or to raise her hand. When students were required to read reports to the class, Mary asked a friend to read her work because she was embarrassed of her accent.

The Martinez family developed an expanded community around the church and school, one beyond their aunts and uncles, many of whom had returned to Mexico the same year that the family settled in Houston. While Mary was close to her sisters, especially Geneva and Dora, attending church events such as the bazaars held to raise funds for the church and forge community among church members, gave them a chance to meet and play freely with friends in the neighborhood without worrying about speaking English. When money wasn't tight, Zapopan would make cakes to donate for the cake walks and staff booths to assist.

Among Mary's best friends were Mary Fernandez, Mary Lou Hernandez, Delfina Villagomez, Gloria Reyna, Clarabelle Rivera, and Alice Garza, all of whom lived nearby. They would often go to the Rusk Settlement House after school, and in the scorching summer days they would play games. Here, they also learned to dance to popular songs. In the 1930s and 1940s, a full house of nine children was its own entertainment; it had to be as money was scarce. A radio was out of the question for many years and television was for the middle class. To entertain themselves, the Martínez kids played hopscotch and jump rope outdoors with other kids in the neighborhood and with each other. They played jacks, pick-up sticks, hide and seek, and made paper dolls. At night, they played games, cards and checkers. When they moved to a small two-bedroom house, the second bedroom was for the older girls and the younger kids slept in the living room and on a screen-enclosed back porch. The oldest daughter Pura would bring home pretty greeting cards that were out of season at the department store where she worked. Pura liked to call herself sister #1. Before she was old enough to find a job, the second oldest, Socorro, would make sugar candy at home to sell to neighbors. She also would find or make things to hold a raffle as a way to earn money. With a large household, chores were required from all children. Mary washed dishes, swept the floors, hung clothes handwashed by her mom, and ironed clothes for her father and brother.

At a young age, Mary and Dora would get up extra early and go to mass together every morning at Immaculate Heart of Mary church. They both loved the solemnity and serenity that going to church brought to them as they prayed for the safety and well-being of their family and a better future. Dora was fascinated by the nuns at church and loved their habits. Starting at a young age, she began imagining a time when she could join a religious order. In the late 1940s when she had completed high school and was working as a secretary at a downtown business, Dora devised a plan to join the convent of the Sisters of Immaculate Heart of Mary, which had a convent in Houston. She kept her intent to join a secret with the exception of telling Mary. Despite her commitment to join, she feared telling her mother because when Dora had once expressed an interest in the convent her mother had been very upset and discouraged her. She wanted her daughters, all of them, to have a life full of the love of a husband and children. Dora understood her mother's desire but her definition of happiness for herself was different and included advanced study, a commitment to God, and teaching young children, which she had always dreamed of doing. Knowing that she was going to join when she reached legal age, Dora began packing a suitcase of clothing and other items she would take with her. She kept it under the bed in the room she now shared with Mary and Geneva. She had visited the convent and learned all she needed to know about joining the order and she prayed diligently for the strength to tell her mom about her decision. When she did, her mother burst into tears and pleaded with her not to go.

Dora didn't waver and she entered the novitiate of the Religious of the Sacred Heart of Mary in late 1947. She assumed a new name, Patricia, that symbolized her devotion to God and a new life. She was to be called Sister Patricia by family, friends, and students alike for the rest of her life. She fulfilled her dream to be a teacher and to travel. Although she was stationed in a number of schools, churches, and shrines throughout South Texas, she traveled to trainings and conferences throughout the United States, visited the home of the order in Beziers, France, and went to the Vatican, as well as Scotland.

Upon completing elementary school, Mary attended Edison Middle School for seventh and eighth grades and then graduated to Milby High School, a few miles walk from home. In the summer between ninth and tenth grade, Mary started working at *La Moderna,* a local grocery store. She was 14. There she waited on customers. She worked from 7:00 a.m. to 6:00 p.m. and was paid $15.00 per week. Since the family was in dire need of money, all but three dollars was handed over to her mother each payday. For entertainment on the weekends, Mary enjoyed going to the movies, skating, or renting a bicycle for a dime an hour and riding to the park to watch a baseball game. There at the park, the girls would watch their boyfriends play as they represented their social group. This social group was called Magnolia Club. They held many parties. "One year," Mary recalled, "we worked very hard to save money to be able to make a trip to Wharton, Texas, in order to play in a baseball tournament. We made the trip and lost but we still had a lot of fun. As we were about to leave, we decided to stop and eat, prejudices were part of the culture and when we entered a restaurant the manager approached us and said, 'We don't serve Mexicans around here.' So, we found another restaurant in a Mexican neighborhood that served us."

Money was so scarce that holidays gifts were non-existent in the Martinez family except for what Zapopan could get delivered from Goodfellows, a holiday charity started in 1911 by the *Houston Chronicle* city editor, George Kepple. Mary recalls:

> *We would always be so excited because my mother couldn't afford to buy us any gifts at all. But treats and gifts would come in from the schools. I remember someone from Edison leaving us a big basket of groceries with fruit and all kinds of things. I remember this big candy cane and mama cut it in pieces. But then the Goodfellows would come in and it would be all these little toys in there and a broom and dishes and dolls. But when we went to the city auditorium a guy that owned theaters would have a program for the poor. And everybody went there and when the program was over they would give you a bag of toys according to age. We went and they gave me this bag and I was so excited because they gave me a real pretty doll. But then when I got home, my sister who was working for this lady that had a little girl, she said, "Well, I'm gonna take it so I can give it to the lady for her daughter," and my mother didn't say anything. And since she was my older sister, I couldn't say anything either. And I just felt real sad, because there goes the only doll that I ever had that wasn't a paper doll. But she actually just wanted to please her boss.*

In high school, Mary joined the drill team. She loved the dance routines, the uniform, and most of all the twirling and tossing of the baton. She also played the bugle. And every Friday they had a game and they had to figure out how to get to the game near downtown. Most of the time she took a bus with a large group of kids. They went out of town to play a few times but her mother never let her go on those trips. She did play in parades in downtown Houston. Around the same time, when she was 15, she started using lipstick. Her mother taught her how to sew so she could make her own drill team uniforms. Later, she would learn to embroider from her mother as well. Mary and Joe's relationship evolved from friendship to dating in high school. They would go on picnics, to the movies, or dances. While they enjoyed traditional Mexican music, they also liked the big band sounds of Harry James, Glen Miller, and Nat King Cole. Mary graduated in 1947 and began working full-time in Sears's credit department as a clerk at the Harrisburg and Wayside location. When she and Joe married in 1952 and moved to a nearby neighborhood, the one where I was sixth-born in 1960, they were one of the first Mexican American families in Denver Harbor. By the time I was a pre-teen, white flight had left the neighborhood majority ethnic Mexican with a few whites and African Americans. In many respects, this was a phenomenon that characterized the transformation of the inner city and the development of the suburbs resulting from post–World War II GI Bill redlining by the banks and the housing industry. From my parents' perspective, they saw Denver Harbor as a "newer" neighborhood just three miles south of Magnolia Park and three miles east of downtown Houston; although it had once been labeled Podunk, Texas by Anglo residents of the neighborhood because of how much they felt isolated from the rest of the city. According to a 2007 *Houston Chronicle* article "The whimsical name faded long ago as the working-class white population filtered out and a working-class Hispanic population filtered in."[iii] Upon the land, where temporary housing for war veterans was placed, McReynolds Junior High was being built. This brand-new school opened its doors in 1958. Resurrection Catholic Church with an elementary school was also just a few

Image 16   Mary Mendoza Milby High School graduation picture, 1948. Mendoza family archives.

blocks away. In the years to come, both of these schools would be important sites of education for their children.

José Mendoza, Jr

María and José Mendoza adapted well to life in Magnolia when they settled there in the early 1930s. After living in a couple of places in the neighborhood, the Mendozas bought a small wood framed three-room shotgun house at 7925 Canal St. in the mid-1930s. The house was near a railroad track, and beyond the track was the Ship Channel where the Mendoza family could see the jumbled masts of ships and hear the deep sonorous bellows caused by the trains and ships as they navigated the narrow paths to places where they would be unloaded and reloaded to serve the industry of a port that was quickly growing to be one of the largest in the country. The Mendoza boys would often play in the field next to the house. Their mother allowed them to wander the small open field but forbade them to ever cross the street. Her fears for their safety were later borne out when Joe was in elementary school. One day his eight-year-old cousin Robert, who went to school with him and lived on the other side of the tracks off Navigation Boulevard, was crossing the tracks to go to school. The shortest path of travel required that he cross the tracks. Sometimes they were confronted with an unmoving train that was waiting in line to be loaded or unloaded. When this occurred, they either crawled under or over the train. One day as he was crawling underneath a train stopped on the tracks, it started to move and cut off his leg. He wore an artificial leg for the rest of his life, but he had a successful career as a truck driver.

Despite the futility of his earlier efforts to be an altar boy, José Jr maintained his closeness to the Catholic Church. He enjoyed the somber, almost mystical feeling produced by the mysteries of the faith and the fervent mumblings of the faithful in the pews. He found the lessons learned from biblical stories and the message of the priests' sermons suited his experience of life—it could be hard, but if you persevered through challenges, struggles, even unfairness, it could be glorious. Perhaps because he seemed more serious and inclined to order and self-discipline, José found himself thinking about the kind of life he wanted. He saw life as an obstacle course to be overcome. While he wasn't yet sure what profession he would pursue, he thought often of the journeys his parents had taken to arrive where they were. His mother spoke about her parents with deep love and respect. She was sad when she spoke of her childhood home in Parras de la Fuente. For a while, during her childhood, they had led a charmed life in a peaceful but important town of the region. Her father had been a respected driver for the Maderos, an important family in the region who had sacrificed a son for the benefit of the nation, and they were surrounded by family members. His father's story was much vaguer and more unclear; there were no known relatives on the Mendoza side.

José's mother had let him know that she and her sisters had been sent to the north for a safer and better life. While they worked hard to provide that for their children, María wanted success for her children, and she felt her children would be the real beneficiaries of her parents' vision of her life in the United States. While she found life in the United States confusing, especially outside of Magnolia, María did try to instill a strong work ethic in their children. While she wasn't certain what kind of financial stability a good education might bring, she did know from her father and her husband that with a strong work ethic, much was possible. When any of her children were past sixth grade and no longer wished to go to school, she did not discourage them from quitting so long as they went to work. To add to the family's pantry, María raised chickens and grew orange and pear trees in their yard. During the Depression, Joe and Mary recalled that because their houses on Canal were near the docks, day laborers who sought work but didn't get any would go by and ask their mothers for something to eat. Their mothers would make them a taco with whatever they had available: potatoes, chorizo, or beans.

María recognized that each of her children was very different; each had their own interests, sense of fashion, and way of interacting with the world. They all kept their hair neatly coiffed. Joe liked a formal style and so he dressed in suits and ties when the occasion called for it. He never thought of himself as better than others so even if he was dressed in a suit, he liked to stop and talk to the pachucos[iv] hanging out at the doors of nearby *cantinas* as well as other men coming home from work with their clothes all soiled. It was a habit he formed when in middle school when he would go to mass on Thursday evenings for Holy Hour, which he would attend regularly. He said, "I would walk from home to the church and there were guys hanging around 76th St. outside the *cantinas*. I used to stop and talk to them there and they knew that I was going to go to church, so when I would leave, they'd say 'Joe, pray for me too.'"

José saw early on that one had to approach the world with one's eyes wide-open. Life with family and friends could be relatively easygoing, but there was always a sense that outside the house, other forces were at work. Speaking English and learning from English language books in which the complexity of the world, its various cultures, and languages were not present, made him feel invisible sometimes. After a few years in school, José became Joe, just as his sister Margarita became Margaret, and his brothers Juan, Roberto, and Jesús became Johnny, Robert, and Jesse.

He and his brothers saw the weekends as a time to make money, be it shining shoes at stores, at the park where Spanish-speaking baseball teams competed, finding a particular corner as evening approached and nighttime revelers were just heading out and still had a few pennies for a shine. With his father's help, José made himself a shoebox out of scrap lumber. It was just big enough to hold cleaning rags, brushes, shining cloths, some shoe wax, and a few color dyes. Between this and selling newspapers in many of the same venues as where he shined shoes, José and his brothers managed to bring in a few dollars every weekend. With the exception of a few coins that they were allowed to keep, their profits went to their mother to help with household expenses. Joe got his first hourly job at a grocery store where he stocked the shelves and made deliveries on a store-owned bicycle. The job made him feel important, especially when food was so precious to people in hard times and employment was inconsistent. Even though times were hard, in the summer of 1941 his mother took him and his brothers to visit her family in Parras. It was only the second time she had returned since initially arriving, and the first with her children. They traveled by bus, train, and car. The boys thought it was an adventure; Parras seemed so small compared to Houston. When they returned, Joe (as he was mostly called in school these days) was happy to live in a much larger city where life seemed more interesting and opportunities to advance one's station in life seemed more abundant than in Parras. Parras had been beautiful, but people seemed to get by on so little money and food. Priests would only show up to town every few weeks and medical attention was almost nonexistent except in the most dire circumstances.

In search of a way to make something happen to help their family survive the Depression, Joe and his brothers went to the docks looking for jobs. With the USA's entry into World War II in December of 1941, the shipyards and train yards exploded with activity on behalf of the war effort and many men enrolled as soldiers. My dad said, "I was only about 13 years old, and I went over to the shipyards. And they asked me, 'How old are you?' I said '17'. They didn't ask to see ID. You told them you were 17 and they would hire you. No proof needed. It was hard work. Hot as could be inside the ship where things were tossed down to us and we packed the ship. I did that several summers during the war when school was out." Joe's oldest brother Johnny quit school to work full-time in the shipyards.

Magnolia Park coming of age

Following the lean years of the Depression, the population of ethnic Mexicans in Houston increased in the early 1940s, as war-related jobs drew Mexican Americans to Houston from across the southwest. The Ship Channel, the railroad industry, and manufacturing boomed as a result of the war effort. Mary recalls that though they sometimes went downtown, they mostly stayed in Magnolia to shop and socialize where there was plenty for them to do with youth clubs, volunteer work, recreational activities at Mason or Hidalgo Park, church activities, and dancehalls. This had the added benefit of minimizing the chance of conflict with Anglos in parts of town where Mexicans were not welcome and might encounter stares or slurs. The Mexican population only grew by 5,000 between 1930 and 1940. According to De León, however, while population growth was minimal, cultural growth abounded. He notes that by 1940, Magnolia Park was a self-contained barrio where residents could find anything they could in Houston's downtown commercial district (De León, 1989).

Joe attended Milby High School and graduated in May 1948 when he was 19 years old. He was the only one in his family to get a high school diploma. In high school he had friends from many different backgrounds. While some white kids taunted him, he chose to focus on "turning the other cheek," and staying out of trouble. Even as a teenager, he took his appearance seriously and tried to dress nicely without being too outlandish. In his junior year he joined the yearbook committee. When he turned 18 in December 1946, Joe promptly registered for the draft as he was required to do. Although World War II was over, conflict in East Asia was brewing and he felt certain he would be drafted. As he registered, he vowed to join the service of his choice before being drafted took any semblance of choice away from him. He decided he would join the army soon after graduation. The veteran benefits would help him pay for college and buy a house when he was ready. Eager to show their loyalty to the USA despite racial taunts and whispers by Anglos that they were not real Americans, many, many young men of Mexican descent joined all branches of the US military during World War II, the Korean War, and Vietnam.

Over the years, since junior high school, Joe had become friends with Mary Martinez from down the street. They had also attended elementary school together and now that they were in high school, he wanted to date her. He found her sweet and pretty, if not a little shy. Over the years, he often saw Mary and her sister Dora at church and they would walk home together—first, by default, by virtue of going in the same direction, but then they began talking and joking with each other. While his was mostly a family of boys, Mary's was mostly girls with one younger brother.

Image 17 Joe Mendoza, Jr. Milby High Senior Photo, 1949. Mendoza family archives.

Walks to and from school eventually led to weekend dates with Dora serving as their chaperone. Mary had been hesitant to say "yes" when it was clear he was asking her on a date because she wasn't sure it was right to date someone younger than her. He had been born in December 1928 and she more than an entire year sooner in early December 1927. Joe even appealed to her younger brother, also named Joe, to convince him to help get Mary to say "yes." With her brother Joe's and sister Dora's approval, alongside her own judgment of his character considering he went to church on his own, she figured he was good and trustworthy. Unlike many, Joe's parents had a car and he had learned to drive it and was allowed to use it on the weekends when his older brother, Johnny, didn't get to it before him. Going to the movies and afterward to James Coney Island for hot dogs was one of their favorite dates. Once, when he had a weekend off, he took Mary and her mother on a picnic to the San Jacinto Monument just on the other side of Deer Park. He forgot to look and, on the ride home, he ran out of gas! He dealt with it right away by getting out and hitchhiking a ride to a gas station. While this was very embarrassing, his future mother-in-law was impressed with his calm demeanor and the speed with which he addressed the problem. On Fridays Joe would drive Mary, her mother, and one of her sisters over to her sister Esther's to watch wrestling matches on TV.

Joe was inducted into the army on December 8, 1950. He was honorably discharged still on active reserve on December 7, 1952. He had been fortunate enough not to be shipped overseas as part of the Korean conflict. While he went to Fort Benning in Georgia for basic training, most of his time was spent stationed at Fort Hood in Killeen, Texas. Joe's intelligence and organizational skills led him to be assigned as a supply sergeant. In this job he ordered supplies and maintained his regiment's stock of food, ammunition, clothing, and other supplies. While he was never overt about it, he liked the authority this position gave him to help ensure the troops were ready for any contingencies that might arise.

When he had long leaves, he would hitchhike home to visit Mary and family. In letters to Mary, he often talked about them getting married and his dreams for the future. After a long and slow courtship throughout high school, Joe and Mary were married

Image 18   Joe and Mary Mendoza circa 1950. Mendoza family archives.

on July 13, 1952 at Immaculate Heart of Mary Church. She was 24, and he was 23. Mary had been nervous that Joe was taking so long to propose, so earlier that year she had delivered an ultimatum to him that they would either get married or break up. That weekend he got a ride to Houston from Fort Hood in Killeen and proposed! Unlike many other men who married when they joined the military as a way to express their commitment and intentions to their fiancée, Joe had always been concerned with being in the best position possible to provide for his new wife and family that was sure to follow. It was a fairly big wedding with Mary's sisters and best friends serving as bridesmaids. That

Image 19   Joe Mendoza in uniform at Fort Hood, circa,1951. Mendoza family archives.

night as they made plans to travel to San Antonio the next day for their honeymoon, David Castillo, the husband of Mary's older sister Socorro, came by the party being held at Mary's parent's house on Canal and told Joe that he had rented them a room at the swanky Shamrock Hilton Hotel near Hermann Park as a wedding gift.[v]

When Joe returned from the army in the fall, he and Mary searched for a home right away in a neighborhood not too far from their parents where many young couples from Magnolia were looking to start their families. With a $500 down payment that they had both saved up for, they bought a two-bedroom

Image 20   Joe and Mary Mendoza, wedding day, 07/13/1952. Mendoza family archives.

house at 935 Hoffman Street. To afford it, they had to assume a mortgage and get a second one to pay a previous owner, so for several years they had two mortgages for a combined total of $65 a month. At that time, Mary remembers that she was making about $40/week as a clerk at Sears. Joe worked at the post office sorting mail, and he was going to night school to acquire bookkeeping skills. He felt that this built on his skills he had developed as a supply sergeant in the army. The next year, he got a tip from an acquaintance about a job with NL Baroid, an oil testing and materials company.

Initially, his job was to keep track of costs associated with product development. After a few years, he decided he wanted to go work for the accounting department in the main office. He mentioned this to his supervisor who told him to go see the comptroller. He did so and a week later he was reassigned to a job in the accounting department. There, he was fortunate enough to meet Cliff Wall, a man who trained him and with whom he worked for much of his 44-year career at Baroid. Joe's pursuit of a degree in accounting at night school ended when he felt it necessary to heed Mary's plea for more help at home in the evenings. Years later Joe would lament not finishing his degree. He witnessed many newly minted certified public accountants get higher paying jobs than him. He was the person often assigned to train these young graduates. He often noticed how they were unable to communicate their ideas in writing and he would tell his children how important it was to be able to express themselves clearly in writing.

When Joe began his job at NL Baroid in 1952, he recalls being the only non-white person in the office. While he said he experienced very little outright discrimination, there were definitely microaggressions by support staff and peers. His primary way of dealing with these was to simply ignore people's behavior. He remembers one female staff member who used to make faces when he came around. This lasted, he said, for many years until she realized he was not going away, and he gave her no reason to continue her behavior as he maintained a polite and professional demeanor. Mary's brother-in-law worked as a salesman at Baroid and they both recalled that he experienced overt and covert discrimination.

Mary shared a story of how her brother-in-law responded to being called a stereotypical name: "He said some of the guys there would start calling him Pancho, and he said: 'Look, I have a name my name is David and I want to be called by my name not by any other name.' And so, once he said that, they stopped calling him Pancho because he told them right from the very beginning that he didn't want to be called that." To this story, my father added: "Yeah, they tried to call me Juan, but I looked at them right in the eye and I said my name is Joe. Can you pronounce Joe? Can you pronounce Joe? He didn't know what to say! Hahaha!" Mary also recalled various anti-Mexican microaggressions she experienced.

> I remember when I was working in the credit department at Sears, it was in 1951. During the lunch hour we would sit down in the ladies' lounge, and one of the ladies there was talking and saying that she went swimming. And she said, "Well, I don't like to go swimming at Mason Park. There's too many Mexicans there." It just hurt me when she said that. I couldn't say anything back to her. It just choked me up. I had a white friend who was real close to me. She was a Catholic and she was really nice. And she said, "Oh, I go there all the time."
> I just got up and went to the restroom and I didn't say anything at all. And then I think they noticed that she worked in the same office. And so, when I got back to the office, she came back up there, and she told me she was sorry. She said: "I didn't mean you." My friend came up to me too and apologized for what the other lady said. Well anyway, the one who said that ended up getting laid off. The lady that I worked for, my supervisor, was a really nice lady. She was the one that got me to

work there typing in the office. She was off on that day but then when she came back the next day, some of the ladies told her. I think my friend was probably the one that told the superintendent about what the girl had said.

To this anecdote from Mary, Joe responded: "They used to say things like that without thinking. I remember one time when a guy would say something about Mexicans and all that and I looked at him and said, 'Do you have a problem with that?' 'Oh no, no, I was just mentioning.' And you know, when you would put them on the to spot like that most of the time they stopped. You had to be direct and talk like that."

On another occasion, Mary almost lost her job when the woman who supervised her went on vacation. While her supervisor was gone, her substitute, a man, moved Mary from her position with no justification and assigned an Anglo woman to that role. Mary was sad and confused, but when her female supervisor returned, she gave Mary her job back because she thought she excelled in that role.

Confronting the source of aggression was difficult and risky. Mary also shared the following:

> There was another time on the bus when I was going to work and these two ladies they were talking about some of the Mexican kids and what they did and she said 'Oh, those Mexicans, that's all they're good for!' I wanted to say something, but I just couldn't. I guess my mother used to tell us not to fight and I didn't know what to say. I just let it go. But then I heard from one of the other ladies because they saw that I didn't talk or say

anything. They knew I worked there. I think they both worked at Sears, too, down on the sales floor. So, they must have told somebody. They said that they thought I was Italian, and didn't mean to hurt my feelings. Anyway, it hurts when people say things like that.

To this, Joe replied: "It wasn't necessarily discrimination but just the way they talk to you or ... You could sense it, you know?" While Joe and Mary acknowledged racial microaggressions and outright discrimination from some businesses and people, they also acknowledged that there were many good Anglos who supported and befriended them. Mary's recollection of her mother's admonition that she should not cause trouble was likely an important strategy for survival. Being evasive, if not invisible, was a way to avoid undue attention to oneself and, in this manner, one avoids conflict, legal trouble, and potentially dealing with the psychological and physical violence inflicted on them.

Mid-century Houston

Despite being a war based on racial injustice, ethnic Mexicans in Houston found that they faced intensified racial discrimination in the workplace during World War II. Advocacy groups such as LULAC used a rhetoric that took the moral high road to critique companies that had discriminatory pay and hiring practices.[vi] Houston's first World War II victim on the battlefield was a Mexican American, a naval fireman from the northside. Two warships built at the Houston shipyard were named after Mexican and Latin American statesman, the SS José Navarro (a signer of the Texas Declaration of Independence) and SS Benito Juarez.

In the post–World War II period, the Cold War brought suspicion of anyone critiquing social policies or employment practices, including that of Jim Crow. Conformity and consensus went hand-in-hand with conservatism. The result was that Mexican Americans faced severe pressure to yield to mainstream culture even as they maintained an attachment to their culture.

From 1940 to 1960, Houston's Mexican descent population almost quadrupled from 20,000 to 75,000 (De León, 1989). By 1960, only 9 percent of Houston Mexicans were foreign-born. Mexican barrios began growing in several other parts of the inner city that were an expansion of or adjacent to barrios in the north and east. Denver Harbor was one of these.

In his book-length studies of Mexican Americans in Houston, historian Arnoldo De León asks important questions about the path and rate of acculturation of Mexican immigrants in Houston and the degree to which variables such as urbanization, economic opportunity, and Americanization influence everyone in a community similarly. De León responds to these questions by stating that his book demonstrates that the "Houston Tejano community has historically exhibited diverse, sometimes conflicting nationalist, class, and ethnic sentiments. Cultural change does not affect everyone in the same form. Degrees of acculturation have ranged a wide gamut."

In considering the status of Mexican nationals and Mexican Americans in mid-twentieth century Houston, the Mendoza and Martinez families provide a good barometer for the obstacles and opportunities available to first-generation immigrants. At least some family members in each of their families had earned a high school diploma. My father and his sister were the only ones in their family, while his siblings went on to join the air force, the navy and the army and entered the work force as an appliance worker, a security guard, and a dock worker. Margaret secured a job at the luxury department store, Sakowitz, in downtown Houston. In Mary's family, three of the nine children finished high school and two went on to college.

As the children of immigrants, the Mendoza and Martinez children were fulfilling their parents' dreams in getting better jobs, often ones that were less hard on the body than the physical work of the mines and fields. As they got married and began their own families, they were all able to buy homes. While many of them stayed in neighborhoods near Magnolia, others ventured further away to Houston suburbs outside of the inner city. Their decisions about where to move as they started their new families were guided by several factors: (1) a "good" neighborhood, one that had good schools, and where they could feel safe and connected to their neighbors; (2) proximity to their parents; and (3) affordability as determined by their ability to get financing.

Historically, residential planning in Houston has been something of a hodgepodge of policies. On the one hand, Houston is notorious for its lack of zoning policies to separate home and business spaces. On the other hand, it has a long history of allowing laws that have limited where certain people can or cannot live. A July 2016 *Houston Chronicle* article (Babinck, 2007) notes that "Houston remains the only major city without a zoning ordinance to regulate which pieces of land can be used for what purposes, despite three major attempts over the past century to bring it in line with the rest of urban America."[vii] A closer examination of redlining and deed restrictions reveals how these practices may have started out with noble intentions but became tools for social control. During the Great Depression, the federal government created the Homeowners Loan Corporation (HOLC) to assist homeowners struggling to keep their homes during the Depression. By 1933, when HOLC was founded, half of all mortgages in the USA were in default. "The agency was charged with bailing out homeowners at risk of default on their mortgages, and, by 1936, more than one million loans had been issued" (Rogers, 2016). See also Guillen (2019) and Schuetz (2019). To assist it in making decisions about the feasibility of loans, in 1935 HOLC created what they called Residential Security Maps. The goal of the maps was to "graphically reflect the trend of desirability of neighborhoods from a residential viewpoint." Below is the visual key used to describe the status of various neighborhoods.

According to Susan Rogers, the author of "The Maps and Loans Behind Houston's Segregation,"

> The power of the maps was to make discriminatory practices visible and provide a verb for the practice of denying loans to certain areas of our cities—an act we now know as "redlining." Specifically, redlining refers to the grading system of the HOLC where "hazardous" areas were colored in red. There were three other grades highlighted on these maps: "definitely declining" in yellow; "still desirable" in blue; and "best" in green. The grades were established based on location, housing age and value, presence of incompatible uses, such as commercial or industrial—and race. (2016)

Hillier writes: "On the one hand, HOLC provided assistance to a million homeowners, across race and ethnicity, who were desperate to save their homes. On the other hand, [it] created security maps in which race was used to signify risk levels."

The 1940 HOLC-generated map of Houston shows how the "redlining" of Houston's real estate map operated in defining for generations to come the potential worth of various neighborhoods. The circled area is Magnolia Park. The area in a rectangle is Denver Harbor, a neighborhood that evolved from the combining of two preexisting neighborhood additions, Harbor and Denver. Most of the remaining areas identified as red, or definitely hazardous, are mostly populated by African Americans. These neighborhoods include the Fifth and Sixth Wards as well as Cottage Grove and the West End.

Since the creation of these maps, Houston has tried several times to institute zoning laws, but these efforts have been met with fierce resistance by people who viewed it as government meddling, calling land-use restrictions "socialistic and communistic." The negative impacts of these maps on loans and suburban planning that led to white flight was further compounded by those who saw how they could be useful in creating deed restrictions that limited transference and purchase of property by race. Although race-based restrictions were struck down in a US Supreme Court ruling in 1948, they have contributed to housing disparities that exist today and still remain in many older associations' documents.[viii] These[ix] maps also played a prominent role in protecting the value of property in white neighborhoods in other ways. For instance, when decisions regarding the placement of interstate highways were being made, it was determined that

102   (Re)Constructing Memory, Place, and Identity

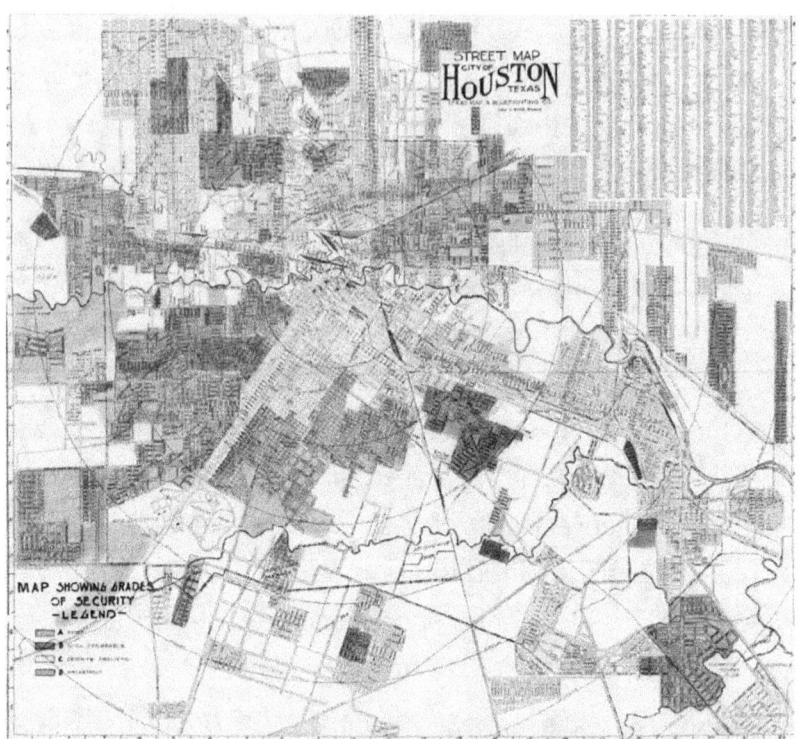

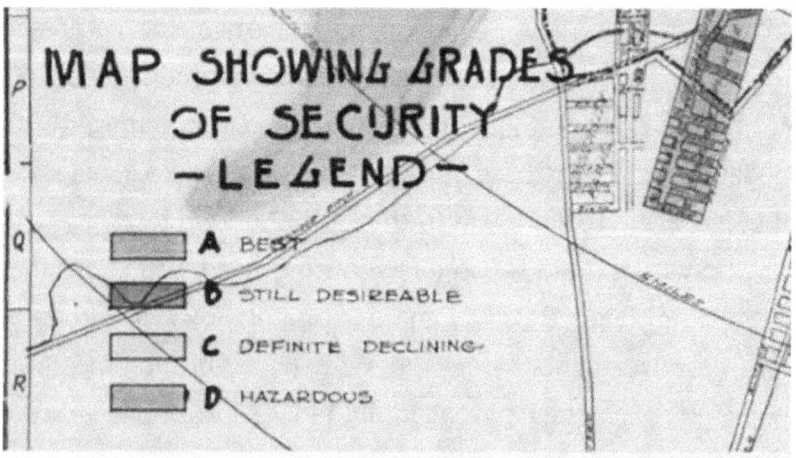

Image 21   "Mapping Inequality." 1940 HOLC Map of Grades of Security of Houston neighborhoods. Enlarged map legend is to left.

the best way to protect high-value neighborhoods was to route the highways through the poorer neighborhoods occupied by African Americans and Latinos (Susaneck, 2018).

∗∗∗

Racial covenants: Though they varied in wording there are numerous examples of language restricting the occupation of a dwelling by non-whites. Below is one example.

> *No person of any race or nationality other than the white race for which the premises are intended, shall use or occupy any building on any lot, except that this covenant shall not prevent occupancy by domestic servants of a different race or nationality employed by an owner or tenant nor shall it prevent occupancy by members of the family of said domestic servants.*

∗∗∗

Like many Americans in the post-War era, the Mendoza family thrived in a strong economy. Joe and Mary became deeply involved in Resurrection Parish as active churchgoers, supporters of the church through their weekly gifts, parents of children attending elementary school there, and participating and assisting in church activities such as bazaars to raise funds for the church or school. A year after their marriage, their first daughter was born and christened Rosemary. Two years later, a second daughter, Mary Ann, was born, followed by a boy in November 1956. Two more girls, Beatrice Marie and Mary Margaret, followed by a second boy Louis Gerard, were born in 1958, 1959, and 1960. A child was stillborn in 1962, and then a fifth daughter was born in June of 1963, Cynthia Marie. Sometime around 1965 Mary miscarried another child when she fell off a bench when the family was visiting Six Flags of Texas in Dallas. Finally, the family was rounded off with the birth of the sixth daughter and eighth child, Mary Gilda, in January of 1967. After the birth of Mary Margaret, who was called Margie within the family, the family needed more room for their growing family, so they moved from the house on Hoffman to a larger house at 615 Zoe St. Around this time, Joe taught Mary how to drive. With five kids and a sixth on the way, the likelihood of needing to drive kids to the doctor, to school, or to go shopping during the week was high.

When Joe and Mary began having children, they discussed their dreams for them, and how they would raise them. One issue that arose that caused some tension with the in-laws was their decision to not raise their children to speak Spanish. Zapopan was more understanding than María. In fact, she had sent her youngest daughter to a different school, one with less Mexican American students, so she could learn to speak English without an accent. María argued with Joe about this decision and lamented that they would not know their mother tongue and would only have a limited ability to communicate with her since she did not speak English fluently. Having survived taunting and humiliation and the shame of not speaking English in schools, Joe and Mary wanted to spare their children this traumatic experience. Perhaps even more importantly, in the 1950s, President Eisenhower's Director of the INS, Joseph Swing, designed and implemented Operation Wetback to deport undocumented Mexican immigrants.[x] Using military style tactics, Operation Wetback successfully deported more than a million people to Mexico, many of whom had legal status in the United States as citizens or visa holders, even though recruitment of Mexican workers continued in the agricultural and manufacturing industries in the Southwestern and Midwestern United States (Rhinehart, and Kreneck, 1988). This followed and coexisted with the Bracero Program (1942–1964) that recruited Mexican laborers to deal with a labor shortage in the agricultural and railroad industries in wartime. Under this program, special visas were issued to allow Mexican migrants to come and work in the USA.

Although they were fully bilingual, Joe and Mary feared that if their children spoke Spanish first and English with an accent they would be targeted by public officials or treated as second-class citizens. Years later, as Spanish gained prominence as a language of commerce and business, they expressed regret for this decision, but they did what they thought was right at the time.

Joe and Mary kept the house on Hoffman and rented it out for supplemental income for the next 55 years. Joe also purchased some other rental units in the near North Side on Gano St. but found that repairs and chasing down tenants who could not pay the rent was not to his liking, so after a few years, he sold them. Mary had quit working when the children entered their lives. She returned to work when the kids were old enough to help around the house. She worked at local department stores, and the neighborhood public library. The latter she did for many years as a reference librarian, where she came to be known by many of the friends of her children. Years later, one of daughter Mary Ann's friends laughingly said that Mrs. Mendoza was Google before Google existed because you could either call in or go visit her in the library and ask her anything and she would look it up and give you an answer right away.

Civil rights, social change, and neighborhood transformation

In the 1960s, Houston youth immersed themselves in the Chicano Movement, much to the chagrin of immigrant families who worried that protests, rallies, boycotts, and strikes would put the community in a bad light. *Papel Chicano*, a Chicano Movement newspaper with offices in Magnolia Park, reported on area activism in the 1970s, and in 1971 women of the Magnolia Park YWCA hosted the Conferencia de Mujeres por la Raza.

Life in the Mendoza home was fairly sedate. Joe and Mary strove for routine and predictability with expectations for meals, school performance, and household chores made clear. As a family, they watched the news and mourned when JFK, MLK, and Bobby Kennedy were assassinated. They watched the news of grim reports on Viet Nam and of the body count of infantry and Viet Nam civilians skyrocketing. They listened to accounts of civil rights and women's rights protests, rallies, and civil disobedience. While Mary and Joe rarely spoke directly about these events, they did not speak against the brazen youth who protested the "man," inequality, and the denial of equal justice for all. Their children participated in small ways in the countercultural movement of the time via their fashion, hair styles, and musical tastes.

Joe and Mary were involved and observant parents as much as they could be with eight children. Homework was critical and each report card required a discussion with Joe as he asked about areas where performance might be low. They did understand that not all of their children were academic high performers but more than anything they wanted their children to have an opportunity to go to college. Joe always told his kids they could be anything they wanted to be, and not to settle for less than that because work was going to be an important part of life. They also wanted their children to work indoors so their bodies would not have to deal with the harsh outdoor climate of Houston. Each evening in the Mendoza household, dinner with the family was mandatory, as were prayers at each meal and church attendance on Sunday. Following lunch on Sundays, family visits to each grandparent ensued. Chores were required throughout the week and especially on Saturday mornings. While some watching of cartoons on television was not uncommon on Saturday mornings, nothing else could be done before all chores were completed. The work was often divided along traditional gender lines, with the girls doing indoor chores like washing dishes, sweeping, mopping, dusting, and vacuuming, and the boys maintained the lawn, painted the house as needed, and raked leaves or washed the car. When Joe was making house or car repairs, one or other of the boys was often drafted as his assistant and, in this way, they picked up car and house repair skills that would last them a lifetime.

The house on Zoe Street was home to the family for 20 years. The block was full of kids who played mostly well together. In the evenings as supper time approached, among the sound of cicadas or frogs chirping in the streets, one could hear the whistles of various tones as parents called their children home to eat. In the early 1970s, Joe and a group of friends added

Image 22 Visiting grandpa and grandma Mendoza, circa 1964. Mendoza family archives.

an upstairs to the three-bedroom house. This two-bedroom addition allowed the older girls, Rosemary and Mary Ann, now in high school, some privacy; the two boys, Bobby and Jerry, took the other room.

A number of scholars have noted that the civil rights movement in Houston was relatively peaceful compared to other sites in the South where resistance to Jim Crow laws was met with fierce violence and vitriol. One example marking this contrast is the violence college students faced in many parts of the southern United States outside of Houston when they held lunch counter sit-in protests. Students from TSU took the lead in advocating and protesting for desegregation. They held sit-ins at restaurants in diners like Woolworths and at the city hall cafeteria. Interestingly, perhaps because they wanted to avoid conflict or because they believed in the cause, many merchants did not resist the sit-ins and served the protesting students. Although the mayor at the time was not supportive of desegregating public facilities, many members of the City Council advocated for desegregation. Additionally, "the Retail Merchants Association, an organization of white business owners, started a campaign to desegregate private businesses throughout Houston. The Retail Merchants Association contacted local Houston businesses with literature outlining not only how it was both economically healthier to desegregate, but how doing so would prevent future violence from developing." ("The East End Then and Now") According to B. Chapman of the *Houston Business Journal* (Chapman, 2007), the city managed to peacefully desegregate lunch counters, hotels, restaurants and movie theaters through a carefully planned process that began in the summer of 1960.

Joe and Mary watched desegregation and were happy to see it take effect. They had always felt uncomfortable having privileges that African Americans did not, even though some businesses applied Jim Crow regulations to Mexicans. Catholic doctrine persuaded them to believe that all people were God's children and disallowed them to see themselves as better than others based on something as superficial as skin color. Joe recalled reading about the sit-ins and how the students stayed put all day, and then a few weeks later, they were being served. He said he did not recall the details, but he did remember that the police stayed out of the fray. He said that in the early 1960s, one slowly started seeing desegregation practices end for restaurants, theaters, water fountains, and pools. Joe was highly involved with the church as a member of the Knights of Columbus and as a volunteer accountant for church fundraising events like biannual bazaars and weekly collections from parishioners. He was also a founding member of the group that helped start the church's credit union for parishioners. In the late 1970s, Senator Edward Kennedy campaigned for president of the United States and he stopped by Resurrection Catholic Church. Joe took a photo.

Joe and Mary could not afford to take the family out to restaurants or go on long vacations, but they did go to Galveston or Lake Houston frequently. Joe loved to travel early and would often get the family up in the dark with the refrain "Rise and Shine, the sun is up and the day is wasting!" Once the kids were treated to a day at the Six Flags of Texas in Dallas. There was also a trip or two to Mexico to visit family who were otherwise unknown to the kids.

Image 23   Ted Kennedy campaigning at Resurrection Catholic Church in Denver Harbor, circa May 1980. Mendoza family archives.

At least a couple of instances when returning from a short trip, the family came home to find that their house had been broken into and robbed. While there were not many valuables in the house, the television and stereo would be gone, and a huge mess created as thieves sought more valuable items perhaps hidden in closets or in pantries. Joe and Mary were very present in their children's lives, but they were not ones to express affection to their children either verbally or physically. The Mendoza children recall with fondness two kinds of indirect intimacy, the annual ritual of looking for *piojos* that Mary conducted before the start of each school year and being carried to their beds when they had fallen asleep in the car or on the couch. Each of these were rare (even as they were routine) moments of tenderness that they reveled in.

The four sides of Denver Harbor were bordered by railroad tracks. Settegast was to the north, Fifth Ward to the west, Port of Houston to the east, and Clinton Park to the south. The high school designated for students from Denver Harbor was Phyllis Wheatley High School on Market Road in the Fifth Ward. Having sent their children to Catholic Elementary school, the Mendozas then sent them to Catholic high schools. When Resurrection Elementary school stopped offering 7th and 8th grades, those who were of age attended Mc Reynold's Junior High before attending Catholic High School. The girls went to Incarnate Word Academy and the boys to St Thomas College Preparatory School. Tuition was a challenge and as each family member got a job when in high school, they were required to contribute to their tuition. Although not in typical fashion, eventually five of the eight Mendoza children earned college degrees. The three others attended, but for a variety of reasons did not complete their studies.

As the girls came of age, several marriages occurred in the 1970s and grandchildren soon followed. While the Mendoza children took advantage of birth control measures that were not easily available or accepted by their parents' generation, all in all Joe and Mary were to have 18 grandchildren and 16 great-grandchildren. In the 1980s, they moved out of Denver Harbor to Woodforest, a suburb near Channelview, Texas, near I-10 East and Beltway 8. Joe and Mary took advantage of retirement to travel, but they remained active churchgoers and volunteers in a number of community organizations until they were no longer able to drive. They were generous, kind, and big-hearted and even when they had a full house of eight children, they opened their homes to several foster children from Catholic charities. After moving to Woodforest, Mary took a job at a local elementary school serving lunches to the children. In the mid-1980s, when her last child, Gilda, left the house to attend college, first in San Angelo and then in San Antonio, Mary experienced a strong case of empty-nest syndrome that lasted several years, and which was accompanied by feelings of isolation and underappreciation. As her numerous grandchildren became old enough to spend time with them, these feelings lessened.

Joe retired for good from NL Baroid Industries in 1996 after working there for 44 years. Around the same time, Mary quit working at the local elementary school in Woodforest where she worked a half-day in the cafeteria. In retirement they kept busy and volunteered as advisers to married couples through a church program, and Joe delivered bread and groceries to elders in the area for a local food pantry. In his 80s, Joe was diagnosed with early-stage Alzheimer's. Though he remained highly functioning for many years, his short-term memory was tasked. In 2016 his children made the difficult decision to take away his car for fear that he would have an accident or forget how to find his way home. He was very upset about this and reacted angrily and kicked them all out of the house when they told him that they had sold it. By the next day he had forgotten about the conversation. From that point on, his children and wife simply told him the car was at the mechanic's being repaired. Although he went looking for it at neighborhood auto repair shops from time to time, this mostly placated him. He loved to drink wine in the evenings and play dominos or checkers with his children and grandchildren.

When Covid arrived in 2020, Joe and Mary stayed home and isolated with only their caretakers allowed to visit them. The six daughters who lived in Houston worked hard for many years to provide for them and visited often as well as taking care of their own family needs and careers; doctor's visits and other responsibilities kept them very busy and the sisters often used vacation and sick days to attend to their parents' needs. Prior to the pandemic, their son Bobby drove in from San Antonio to spend at least one weekend a month with them. Mary had long suffered from osteoporosis and weak bones. In fall 2020 her doctor informed her that her upper jaw bone was decaying and needed a graft. On the one hand, he was very concerned with the risks involved in this procedure, and especially concerned with the heightened risk of exposure to Covid she would face in a hospital. On the other hand, if she failed to get the operation there was an increasing risk that the wound in her jaw would go septic. She decided to have the operation, but it was postponed because of scheduling complications. In January of 2022, Joe and Mary were put under hospice care at home. Soon afterward they were diagnosed with Covid. In addition to their children, many grandchildren visited to say their final goodbyes. Their sons, Bobby and Jerry, were in town and spent the night with them so that their sisters could get some rest. While Bobby slept for a few hours, Jerry could see his mother's breathing becoming labored and anticipated her death so he played a recording of a mass, and some of her favorite music, such as Ave Maria and Volver, in the hopes that this would give her comfort. Mary succumbed and died in the early morning hours of Sunday, January 24th. Joe had not been exhibiting any signs of illness, but once Mary was put in a hospice, he refused to eat and began sleeping on a couch near the hospital bed that had been set up for Mary in the den. At her death, he seemed aware of what had transpired and kept saying he was OK as tears rolled down his face. The next morning, slightly less than 24 hours after Mary died, he passed away. Many of his children believe that he willed himself to go with Mary. He had been saying for years that he was planning on living only as long as Mary did so he could be there for her.

After Joe and Mary passed, the family went through their personal items and a letter from Joe to Mary was found that confirmed his intention to stay by her side to take care of her.

In a note to Mary in July 2011 on their fifty-ninth wedding anniversary, Joe wrote to Mary:

> *My dearest Mary,*
> *I just want to tell you how much I love you and how much you mean to me. I know sometimes you probably think*

Image 24 Joe and Mary Mendoza, circa 1952. Mendoza family archives.

> *I no longer care for you because I don't respond quickly when you want something, but my slow reaction is due to getting old, tired, and sluggish. I pray every day that our Lord will continue to keep me well so that I can help you and take care of you.*
> *I still remember well telling our Lord that if he granted you to be my wife, that I would always take care of you and love you with all my heart as I still do.*
>
> *Joe*

Mary and Joe lived through the Great Depression, and they saw Houston expand from a small city to become Texas's largest and

Image 25   An extended family gathering at Mason Park in the late 60s. Most of my siblings and many cousins are in the picture. I am the one kneeling on the left. Mendoza family archives.

the nation's fourth largest city with only New York, Los Angeles, and Chicago surpassing the population of Houston. They witnessed the exponential growth of the Latino population. Whereas the Mendoza name in Houston once only occupied an eighth of a page in the phone book, it filled many pages by the end of the twentieth century. They experienced the development of running hot water in their homes, the rising popularity of their first radio, then B&W TV, then color television and phones, then cell phones, and then the internet. They saw assassinations and assassination attempts at presidents, presidential candidates, and civil rights leaders. They saw the USA on the brink of World War III with other superpowers. They saw the development of technology that allowed space travel, trips to the moon, and other forms of space exploration. Throughout all of this, they never ceased to be amazed but also believed that nothing was more important than family, God, and treating one another with love and respect.

3
Coming of age in the Space City: cowboys, astronauts and other specters

> *A memoir is a work of sustained narrative prose controlled by an idea of the self under obligation to lift from the raw material of life, a tale that will shape experience, transform events and deliver wisdom --*
> Vivian Gornick, 2002

I have often wondered if my life is story worthy. What does being story worthy mean? To imply that one person's story is meaningful, and another's is not, seems elitist. While I believe every life is meaningful, I think how one assigns meaning to one's life matters. How, then, do we make our lives matter? Is it more meaningful if one's life narrative converges or diverges from those of others? In other words, should we think about what makes us distinct from others or what binds us to them? If this is a gauge for story-worthiness, then we are able to find meaning in our lives only in our relationships with others. Context is everything, for I am nothing outside of my relations with others and the world in which I live.

In the dog days of summer in 1960 in Houston, Texas, "It's Now or Never" by Elvis Presley was number one on the US Billboard Hot 100 charts. Dwight D. Eisenhower was still president, though he would be defeated later that year by the young, handsome, and charming John F. Kennedy. And in response to the United States' embargo against Cuba, Fidel Castro nationalized American and foreign-owned property on the island. If the youth of the 1950s can be characterized as rebels without a cause, the 1960s came to be labeled as a decade of protest and rebellion against dominant cultural and political norms around gender, race, and sexuality, and numerous other social conventions. In fact, my birth date of August 25, 1960, was not only the day the 1960 Olympics in Rome started, it was also the day that Foley's Department Store in Houston voluntarily enacted a new policy of integrating its lunch counters, heralding in a new era of social relations as the desegregation of most other Houston area restaurants followed suit.[i] With a population of approximately 938,000, Houston had climbed from being the eighty-fifth largest city in the USA in 1900 to the nation's seventh largest city, and Texas's largest. By 1990 its rapid growth would make it the fourth largest city in the country, where it continues to rank today. Long seen as the energy capital of the world, this sobriquet for Houston was once challenged by the emergence of Houston as the space capital. The two celebratory monikers coexist in synergistic relationship to one another.

The federal government picked Houston for its Manned Spacecraft Center in 1961. The center opened that year to house the workforce that would develop the spacecraft, train the astronauts, and support the nation's efforts to land a man on the moon and safely return him to Earth by the end of the decade. With it, almost immediately the city embraced a new identity, as Space City, USA. This was soon reflected in local sports team names. The Colt 45s baseball team became the Astros when the team moved to the newly built Astrodome in 1965. The owner of the Astros, Roy Hofheniz, explained the name change: "We felt the space idea was more logical because the ballclub is in Houston – Space City, USA, and our Spring Training headquarters are in Cocoa Beach, Fla., at Cape Kennedy – Launching Pad, USA … The name and insignia will help dispel the image of Texas as a land of cowboys and Indians, and it behooves every citizen in this area to call attention to the twentieth century aspects of Texas and Houston."ii

Other sports franchises soon followed the Astros' lead. The World Hockey Association (WHA) team, the Houston Aeros, were originally slated to play in Dayton, Ohio but ended up coming to Houston instead. Although the Aeros' name had originally been chosen in honor of the Wright brothers, it was seen as appropriate for Houston given the importance of the space industry. Another sports franchise with an appropriate name that was derived elsewhere is the Houston Rockets basketball team. The team was founded as the San Diego Rockets in 1967 and moved to Houston in 1971.

Houston's emergence as the Space City was to have an influence on my perspective, literally, as I and thousands of others of the era found a way to get a telescope in advance of the first moon landing on July 20, 1969. My cousin Jesse and I would stay up late in the backyard and watch the night sky hoping to become so familiar with it that we would be able to easily discern a spaceship moving toward the moon when the time came. Other nights we would climb a tree or situate ourselves on the roof of the garage and check out Houston's growing skyline. From a tall cottonwood tree in our front yard, one could see the rotating Gulf building sign, known as the lollipop, glowing in the distance from three miles away.

Such was the context of my early life in a city that was rife with growth—a bustling economy that was emerging as a force to be reckoned with on the national stage, a southern city that steadfastly maintained traditional elements of white hegemony even as it was emerging as a multiracial society and struggling to adapt. When I think of the numerous influences that shaped who I am, I have to acknowledge the role that primary social institutions, such as family, church, education, media, and police, played in shaping my life and identity. The name one is assigned at birth by family is often simultaneously backward and forward looking as it can reflect one's historical legacy and familial aspirations for a newborn. And so it was the case in my family as the names assigned to my siblings and myself were influenced by familial legacy, religious identity, social relations/context, and popular culture. This can be seen in the names of each of my siblings and myself. In honor of our Catholic heritage each of my six sisters' names contains some variation of María thereby simultaneously recognizing our mother's name of María and in doing so honoring the venerated role of the Virgin Mary/Virgen de Guadalupe in Mexican Catholicism. My siblings' names in order of birth are: Rosemary, Mary Ann, Robert Joseph, Beatrice Marie, Mary Margaret, Cynthia Marie, and Mary Gilda. Their names, including mine, Louis Gerard, reflect an influence by key figures and dates of Catholicism, our parents' social networks of family and friends, and popular culture. For instance, I was born on the feast day of St Louis and not only does my name honor this venerated saint of Catholicism but it also happens to honor the name of both of my maternal great-grandfathers, Luis García and Luis Martinez, even as it also reflects the decision by my parents to adapt to contemporary social pressures of anglicizing our names, a pro-active decision on my parent's part that must have anticipated the inevitable nature of the anglicization of identity that their own names underwent during their childhood. Thus, it was that the twin influences of family and religion conspired to shape my earliest sense of identity and social belonging, though even at a very young age, place and social identity began playing a role that I would not fully understand for years to come.

Growing up Mendoza: hand-me-downs and a close-knit family

A study published in the journal *Memory* in 2021 suggests that most people can retrieve memories from the time they are about 2.5 years old.[iii] This seems about right for me. I have long tried to recall my earliest memory and the handful I come up with are a vague memory of my Uncle David calling me to come to him at a family picnic in a park. I recall being very small, and I have always felt I was around two at the time. The second memory I have is hiding behind the skirts of Grandma Martinez when my parents came to pick me up after they had been on a trip. I clung to her because I was mad and hurt at having been left behind. In her firm, but gentle and loving way, she reconnected me with my parents. Later on, I would learn that they had taken a trip to Mexico together to heal from the loss of a stillborn child and had also left my siblings with other family members. I also have early memories of playing underneath the banana trees on the side of their house; it was a place that, along with the magnolia trees, provided cool shade in the heat of the summer. I recall spending weekends at Grandma and Grandpa Mendoza's house with my cousin Jesse. We played and always obeyed their commands to do this or that chore, and we always felt safe. I also recall my parents saying goodbye as they left our house to go to the hospital for my mother to give birth. My five older siblings and I were in the den of our home watching TV on the evening of Tuesday June 4, 1963 and I remember pleading with my mom, "Please, please bring me a little brother!" My sister Cindy was born the next morning. When I next saw my mother, she said: "I'm sorry son, but they were all out of boys." In addition to faint memories of spending time at home with my mom before starting school, using a chair to stand at the sink and wash dishes, and hanging clothes on the line outside to dry, I have a vivid memory of watching President John F. Kennedy's funeral on television. I recall everyone being sad, my mother crying, and JFK Jr's salute to his father. Having also been born in 1960, I related to this little boy and recall feeling sorry for him.

My parents raised us to believe in the power of education to transform our lives. They asked us to imagine what we wanted to be and told us that an education would help us achieve that goal. Thus, school was always deemed important, as was homework. I recall when I was a youngster my father leaving each morning with a car full of my siblings to drop them off at school. The oldest, Rosemary, was seven years older than me, with Mary Ann being five years older, Bobby, four, Beabee, two, and Margie one year older.

Life in our household was structured, routine, and consistent. Each morning our father woke us up with an energetic call to "rise and shine!" We ate breakfast together just as we did for dinner each night. Most mornings oatmeal and toast were served, though on weekends we occasionally had cereal, eggs, or pancakes. Brownbag lunches of bologna and cheese were routine, although occasionally we received peanut butter and jelly. These, along with fruit, were made in haste each morning. Saturday mornings (after breakfast and some cartoon watching) were all about fulfilling a list of routine and special chores created by my father. Clothes and linens were washed, floors swept and mopped, bedrooms cleaned and organized, the yard raked, the driveway swept, and the cars washed. Only after our assigned tasks had been completed could we go about our day playing games with each other or neighbors or participating in activities out of the house. Each Sunday was structured around attending church and then picking up pan dulce and visiting our grandparents.

These visits were as regular as church. We tumbled out of the station wagon and paid homage to our grandparents, whose small houses smelled like the inside of a cedar chest and were as neat and clean as they were dark and cool. The visits always started off formally with a ritual hug, kiss, and pinch of the cheek followed by a survey of our appearance. We marveled at how these small two-bedroom wood-frame houses had managed to hold our parents' larger families of six and nine children respectively. Invariably, after our grandparents asked us how school was going in their halting English, the conversation between grandma and grandpa and mom and dad would take place almost exclusively in Spanish. Sometimes we stayed listening in amazement at how they could understand each other when it seemed everyone was talking as fast as they could all at the same time. You didn't hear that kind of simultaneous exchange among English speakers. Why was it that the English in our house required that only one person at a time speak? Usually, we drifted off and wandered outside to play in the yard or sit on the porch. Sometimes one or more of us stayed around and let the conversation wash over us like a cool summer breeze hypnotizing us with its rich cadence and often lulling us to sleep because, in truth, though there was something nice about witnessing the exchange of familial intimacies and intricacies of life between the generations, we understood almost nothing being said.

While we did not have a lot of extras in our life, we were not wanting. Hand-me-down clothes within family and between extended family was common. I remember once when one of mother's sisters brought some recently washed used clothes over, I put them up to my nose and breathed deeply because I liked the lingering scent of their laundry soap. My mother thought I was being rude and chastised me. They laughed when I explained why I had smelled them with such vigor. I also remember going with my mother to a warehouse on Old Clinton Drive to pick up government-issued powdered milk, huge blocks of cheese, and sometimes bags of rice. Rice and beans were the staple of most evening meals, as were fresh flour tortillas. My sisters were tasked with helping to make meals and, later when my mother went back to work, taking charge of putting dinner on the table. I do recall fondly the times we formed a production line to make tortillas—one person in charge of the dough, two to roll out the uncooked dough, and another to stand at the grill and cook them. My mother was a home economist extraordinaire. Not only did she diligently shop with coupons at several local grocery stores, mostly Weingarten's and Rice Super Market, but sometimes Trahan's, she managed to provide tasty meals that often contained very little meat. We all noticed that my dad was always served a larger portion of meat than us, but mom explained this as he needed the food because he worked all day. Haircuts were mostly a home affair until we got jobs and could afford to go to the local barber's or salon.

My family called me by my middle name of Jerry. It was not until I was about to start kindergarten that my father sat me down and told me that they might call me Louis at school because that was the name I was registered under. I was confused and said, "Why?" My father explained that my full name was Louis Gerard Mendoza. It was not until I attended high school that I began to be called Louis by teachers and fellow students alike. Until this day, I know that if someone calls me Jerry it is a family member or someone from my childhood in Denver Harbor.

Denver Harbor: The interplay of spaces, institutions, and identity

One Sunday in the spring of 1966, before I started elementary school at Resurrection, my father walked me to church, a rare event as I recall it because we usually went as a family. To get there we walked south a block and a half down Zoe St. and walked over the as yet unopened I-10 freeway. I recall him lifting me over the fence dividing the east and west bound lanes, and he said this would be the last time we should ever walk on the highway because it was scheduled to be opened soon. This interstate highway had been a long time coming. It both connected and divided us from the rest of the world. While we had two exits into Denver Harbor, one at Kress and Lathrop Streets and one at Wayside, the freeway went right through the middle of our neighborhood which was bordered by Liberty Road to the North and Buffalo Bayou just south of Old Clinton Road. Because we were already bordered by railroad tracks on all four sides, which were strategically connected to industrial plants, warehouses, and the water treatment facility, many residents of Denver Harbor were already exposed to intense air pollution. The opening of I-10 only intensified this exposure. As was true throughout the USA, the expressways built in Houston after World War II disproportionately affected communities of color. While it is the case that new "… interstate highways increase mobility in urban areas by reducing travel times for cars, buses, and trucks, while lessening traffic congestion on non-interstate roads, and the addition of the interstate also allowed cities to expand their physical size,"[iv] it is also the case that "these projects have invariably destroyed and displaced whole communities, devastated the tax base of cities while subsidizing suburban commuters, and created unseemly moats of high-speed traffic and polluted air that ruined the urban fabric of city neighborhoods for a generation or more."[v] Members of my family tend to disagree on whether or not the freeway caused a sense of division among residents of Denver Harbor or made us more isolated from the rest of the city. I always thought it did a little of both as the sheer presence of the freeway reminded us that we were part of a much larger city and many neighborhoods had house, parks, stores, and restaurants that were much nicer than ours.

I loved going to church on Sundays where I would see my school and neighborhood friends all dressed up. Like my dad, I was enthralled with the mysticism of the church, and I liked the formality of the rituals and ceremony. Unlike him, as a student at Resurrection Elementary Catholic School I was given the opportunity to be an altar boy. It was a duty I relished into my early teen years. I loved how important wearing a cassock and surplice made me feel, that I was at the center of the action with all eyes watching as I carried the cross down the aisle, held the platter underneath those receiving the Eucharist, rang the bells at just the right moment marking the transubstantiation of wine and host to the body and blood of Christ, lit and put out the candles, and swung the incense during special ceremonies for the dead such as at funerals or Easter.

I was such a reliable altar boy that in sixth grade the parish priest, Father Robert Carlson, asked me to be the lead altar boy, an offer I gladly accepted. What this entailed was making the weekly schedule for all the altar boys on Saturdays and Sundays. I also trained new altar boys and was tasked with ensuring that unblessed host and bottles of red wine were kept in stock in the sacristy. So adept was I at doing this that in June 1973 I was named altar boy of the year for our parish and received recognition at a ceremony at the diocese. My parents bought me a new suit for the occasion. That same day, my sister Mary Ann was honored as the best actress in the Galveston-Houston diocese through the

Image 26 The Mendoza kids with mother outside of Zoe St. home.

Catholic Youth Organization (CYO). We are shown in the picture here with Bishop Morkovsky following the ceremony.

While I was a devoted altar boy, I was not necessarily the most devout Catholic. I attended Resurrection Elementary School in Denver Harbor and received a strong educational foundation, but I was not always a fan of the nuns or the priests stationed at our church. The principal of the school was usually a nun, and teachers consisted of other nuns and some lay people. Discipline was strict and failure to abide by rules came at a price. Sister Dolores, my first-grade teacher, would walk around the room and did not hesitate to conk you on the head with her wooden clicker if you spoke out of turn, chewed gum, or seemed otherwise distracted. Boys and girls received different consequences for

Image 27   Mary Ann and I with Bishop Morkovsky at diocesan award ceremony, circa 1973. Louis Mendoza personal collection.

misbehavior, but they all involved humiliation and/or some form of corporal punishment. In addition to being conked on the head, boys might be paddled. Principal Sister Devota seemed particularly fond of having boys raise their pant legs so she could swat our calves multiple times with a wooden yardstick. Sister Jo Anne Bifano had boys kneel in front of class, place their arms in front of them, and hold ten encyclopedias for half an hour. Of course, they also practiced the age-old punishment of having us repeatedly write a rule we had broken on the chalkboard or a sheet of paper. This was in addition to wearing a dunce hat or drawing a circle on the chalkboard and requiring the students being punished to stick their nose in it for 15 minutes.

I was a good student. By that I mean that I performed well and was often one of the best students in class when it came to learning even if, at the same time, I was not always well-behaved. Excelling in academics gave me confidence that transferred to the playground, playing organized sports, and socializing. Although short in stature, in elementary school I walked and talked with an ease that demonstrated a comfort in my skin. There were times when being a middle child in a big family meant that one craved attention, but I also took advantage of that to explore my inner world, one enhanced by avid reading. I recall that I would get so absorbed in reading that my parents would yell at me to stop because I did not hear their calls for me. On hot summer days, I would find a place to hide, the shaded part of the top of the garage roof or my favorite spot, underneath our raised house. The sides of the house were covered, but there were vents and there was soft, cool sand. I would lay by a vent and while away the time lost in books. Sometime in middle school, when I was still an altar boy and I had not quite yet outgrown my comfort with the role, I started helping myself to small portions of money donated to the church via the poor box or the collection basket. I did not take large sums of money, but enough to supplement my weekly allowance and provide for some spending money to treat my friends to malts or the movies. I rationalized that it was money meant to help poor parishioners, and I was personally poor, although even then I knew our family was not one that needed a handout from the church.

To be fair, every one of my five siblings, excluding the eldest and the youngest, has often talked about growing up with a craving for more affection, attention, and intimacy. My parents were not physically affectionate, nor were they all that vocal about telling us that they loved us, though their every action seemed intent on keeping us safe and secure. Although we children could be loud if left to our own devices, there was an unwritten rule in our household that excesses of any sort would not be tolerated. We could not whine, speak too loudly, laugh too loudly, or even be too quiet without drawing negative attention from our parents. I look back now and it appears that there was an economy of emotion at play in our family in which keeping an even keel was the ideal, and emotional excess threw things off balance in our household.

My mother dealt with minor disciplinary transgressions, but it was my father who addressed those issues that deserved more sustained attention or discipline. The familiar adage of "wait until your father gets home!" was a common refrain in our house, and we often waited with dread for his arrival home from work. Depending on the infraction, we might face a stern lecture, a grounding, or corporal punishment, which was meted out swiftly and in a no-nonsense manner. From my perspective, I recall that it was the boys who were more likely to receive a spanking with a belt, a board selected from wood kept in the garage, or a switch taken from a branch of a nearby tree. Though firm and delivered without hesitation, I never felt as if my father enjoyed doling out corporal punishment. Some time when I was around 13, he took me aside and told me I would no longer be spanked—that we would talk, and I would receive denials of privileges befitting my behavior. This was a great relief to me. Unlike my brother, I never challenged my father directly. My brother was more overt in his defiance of household rules about staying out at night, being present for dinner meals, not speaking back to our parents, and yelling at our sisters. Consequently, he and my father developed a very tense relationship in his teen years, one that often seemed on the brink of erupting into physical confrontation and Bobby began threatening to run away. These very loud arguments frightened me. I saw little evidence of being able to win such a fight, so although I broke plenty of rules when I was a teen, I did not draw attention to my defiance in the way my brother did. I knew from listening to neighbors that some parents lost control when disciplining their children or when arguing with a spouse. I would occasionally hear yelling accompanied by the thud or thwack of skin-to-skin physical confrontation, and I was always thankful that those instances were rare in our house.

Our parents were not our friends. I did not confide in them, nor did I express my fears, desires, or feelings with them. Nevertheless, I grew up a reasonably happy and extrovert boy, and I had no problem asserting myself and getting my needs met in the world, despite the fact that my parents had lots to worry about and often too little energy, time, and emotional and material resources to share with us. We looked to our siblings or outside the home for connection, companionship, and affirmation. I recall playing games with my sisters, everything from jump rope, jacks, or Ring around the Rosie. My brother and cousins and I played army with the plastic soldier figures and the little statuettes of presidents given out at the grocery stores. Later, when our father put a basketball goal on the roof of the garage, our driveway was converted into a neighborhood basketball court where games were held sometimes for days and into the night.

As I noted before, my parents stressed the importance of education and they took the time to make sure we did our homework, discussed report cards with us, asked us to explain why we were not doing better if our grades were low, and rewarded us when we did well. To support their aspirations for us, my father regularly purchased books. He subscribed to *Reader's Digest* condensed books, he purchased sets of encyclopedias every few years, and he bought an entire set (with bookshelf) of *Great Books of the Western World*. While most of us did not read these on a regular basis, I explored works by Tolstoy, Dostoevsky, Shakespeare, and a number of philosophers. Although these were well over my head, I plowed through them with a dictionary in hand. Even then, my comprehension as a middle schooler was wanting; I did read many of these later, but the fact that we owned them signaled that our parents aspired for us to lead literate lives that transcended our sense of place and time in the world.

My father also found secondary uses for the books on our family shelves as well. While my grades were consistently strong in academics, my conduct was sometimes wanting as was my penmanship. Both of my parents had beautiful handwriting. My mother's penmanship was flowing and fancy. One could almost say it was very feminine. In contrast, my dad's penmanship was also very beautiful but highly masculine. You could tell he pressed hard on the paper and used a combination of print and handwriting. It was firm, decisive, and legible. To this day, my handwriting and signature are barely legible, even to me. Several times a year when we received report cards in elementary school and I received a "U" for Unsatisfactory in penmanship, my father would require that I copy a full page out of an encyclopedia or great book for a week, handing them over to him for inspection. Following the principle that practice makes perfect, he thought that writing more often would improve it. It did not. But it did expose me to books and ideas that were heretofore unknown to me.

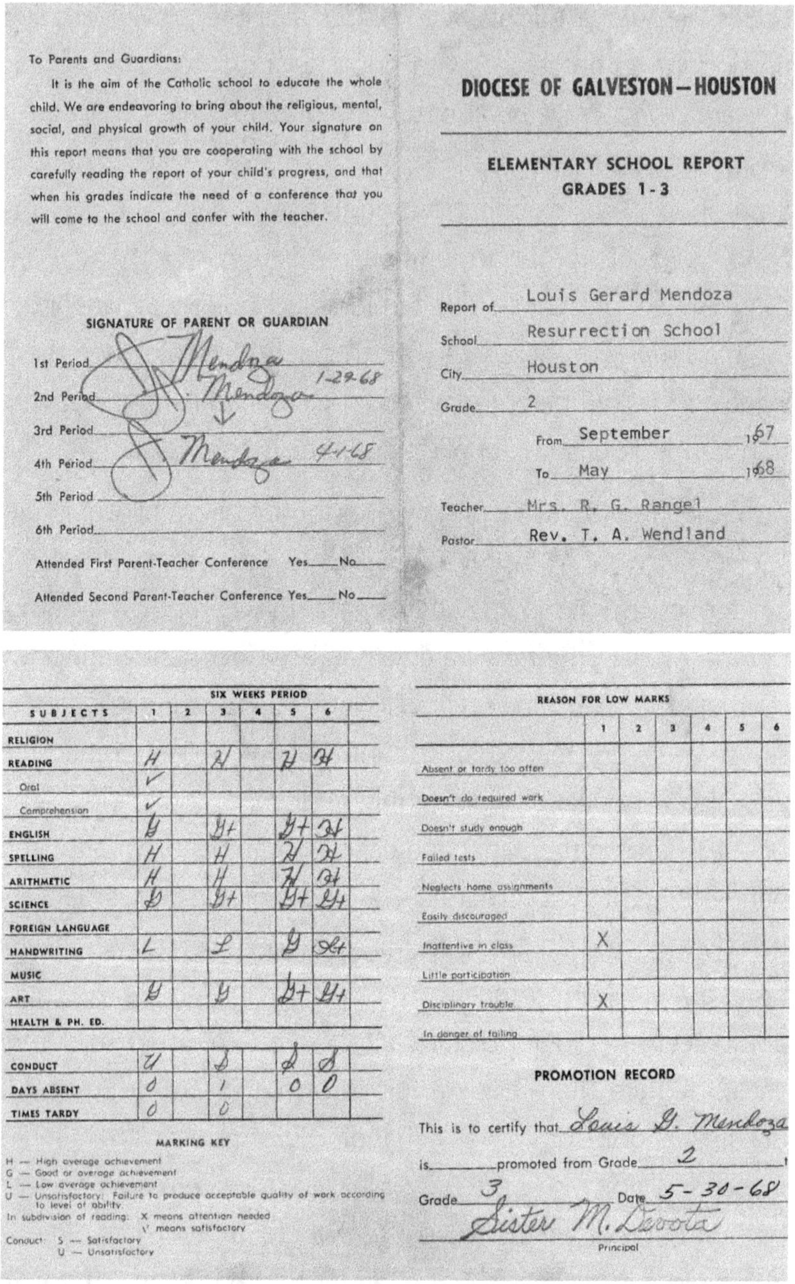

To Parents and Guardians:

It is the aim of the Catholic school to educate the whole child. We are endeavoring to bring about the religious, mental, social, and physical growth of your child. Your signature on this report means that you are cooperating with the school by carefully reading the report of your child's progress, and that when his grades indicate the need of a conference that you will come to the school and confer with the teacher.

SIGNATURE OF PARENT OR GUARDIAN

1st Period Mendoza 1-29-68
2nd Period Mendoza
3rd Period
4th Period Mendoza 4-1-68
5th Period
6th Period

Attended First Parent-Teacher Conference Yes____ No____

Attended Second Parent-Teacher Conference Yes____ No____

DIOCESE OF GALVESTON—HOUSTON

ELEMENTARY SCHOOL REPORT
GRADES 1-3

Report of Louis Gerard Mendoza
School Resurrection School
City Houston
Grade 2
From September 1967
To May 1968
Teacher Mrs. R. G. Rangel
Pastor Rev. T. A. Wendland

SUBJECTS	SIX WEEKS PERIOD 1	2	3	4	5	6
RELIGION						
READING	H		H		H	H
Oral	✓					
Comprehension	✓					
ENGLISH	G		G+		G+	H
SPELLING	H		H		H	H
ARITHMETIC	H		H		H	H
SCIENCE	G		G+		G+	G+
FOREIGN LANGUAGE						
HANDWRITING	L		L		G	L+
MUSIC						
ART	G		G		G+	G+
HEALTH & PH. ED.						
CONDUCT	U		S		S	S
DAYS ABSENT	0		1		0	0
TIMES TARDY	0		0			

MARKING KEY

H — High average achievement
G — Good or average achievement
L — Low average achievement
U — Unsatisfactory: Failure to produce acceptable quality of work according to level of ability.
In subdivision of reading: X means attention needed
✓ means satisfactory
Conduct: S — Satisfactory
U — Unsatisfactory

REASON FOR LOW MARKS

	1	2	3	4	5	6
Absent or tardy too often						
Doesn't do required work						
Doesn't study enough						
Failed tests						
Neglects home assignments						
Easily discouraged						
Inattentive in class	X					
Little participation						
Disciplinary trouble	X					
In danger of failing						

PROMOTION RECORD

This is to certify that Louis G. Mendoza
is_____ promoted from Grade 2
Grade 3 Date 5-30-68
Sister M. Devota
Principal

Image 28 3rd Grade report card. Louis Mendoza personal collection

Despite wanting to expose us to the world through literature, my parents were not always good communicators about sensitive topics. There were certain subjects they actively avoided or only made huge proclamations about that sounded wise but were devoid of a deeper explanation. Sex was one such topic. If sex education remains a hot topic today, it was shrouded in secrecy in the late 1960s, despite the sexual revolution occurring at that time. In sixth grade, Sister Joanne Bifano delivered a unit on the birds and the bees to us. It was done without any direct reference to people or human anatomy, but like much sex education of the time it was a curriculum that focused on species reproduction in the natural world. To be honest, it was not clear at all what we were to take from the lesson about human reproduction, which included an animated film on bees pollinating flowers. In fact, as I recall, mostly what we learned was about plant reproduction with some parallels to animal reproduction with no discussion of human procreation or any anatomical lessons. We were led to believe that we should see parallels in human behavior, but most of us remained mystified and we were too ignorant or embarrassed to ask direct questions because no one seemed to really want to talk about it, especially not the teacher or our parents. One fellow student, Pilar Avalos, asked Sister Joanne how procreation occurred when a man and woman slept with one another since, of course, they were unconscious. Sister Joanne's faced turned beet red, she closed her eyes, and after a few seconds whispered, "God makes it happen." When Pilar asked "How?" Sister replied, "Discuss this with your parents." The evening after our lesson my parents attended a meeting at the school to be informed about what we had been taught, and they were told to come home and ask us if we had any questions. I waited with anxiety thinking that they might come home and have "the" talk with me. When they arrived, they came straight to my room with their coats still on and asked: "do you have any questions about what you learned in school today?" I said, "Hmmm, no?" They both breathed a sigh of relief and said, "well, OK, don't stay up too late," and left the room quickly.

Years later, my oldest sister Rosemary would ask my dad about how he learned the facts of life and he said, "through observation." Although I don't think he meant that literally, I suppose my reality was not too much further from that. In the often overgrown alleyway behind our house, which we boys often took for a shortcut if we were headed to Lyons Street, one or more than one of the neighborhood boys kept stashes of *Playboy* and *Penthouse* magazines, which I often found and perused rather frantically. In the pages of these magazines, I learned more about the human body, male desire, and male heterosexuality than I ever did in a classroom. This is not to say that what I was exposed to wasn't fraught with problems, revolving around the male gaze as it was, I just didn't know any better or have any other options to discuss sex. One day, in the sixth grade, I took one of these magazines to school to share with my male classmates. I stashed it in my desk when we went out to recess and then returned it to its hiding place in the alley on the way home. Later that week, my girlfriend told me that Sister Joanne had pulled her aside and told her to stay away from me because I was a "bad, bad boy!" She did not say why, but I suspect she had found my contraband magazine and was too anxious to confront me or my parents about it.

Denver Harbor in the 1960s was a mixed-race neighborhood, and a very young one. Our street was chock full of young kids our age. Between that and relatives that lived in the neighborhood, we all had plenty of connections outside of our immediate family. Denver Harbor Park and, later, Cliff Tuttle Park, were the focal points of recreation. I started playing baseball in the Pee Wee league of six and under and played Little League and later Pony League, thus baseball was my sport of choice from the age of five through 17. I was not as good as my brother but did well enough to regularly make the All-Star team as a pitcher, catcher, or outfielder. I was inspired by the likes of Pete Rose, Roberto Clemente, and several players in the Houston Astros who I idolized, such as Joe Morgan, Doug Radar, Jimmy Wynn, Cesar Cedeno, and others. Bobby and I were in the first cadre of Astros Buddies when they started in the late 1960s and we would go to games religiously, sometime riding to and from the game on the bus. Sometimes we even walked the ten plus miles home with a group of friends. One time we wandered into the old Colt 45s stadium storage building near the Astrodome and rifled through tossed away memorabilia. We took a circular wooden sign with the Colts' logo of crisscrossed six shooters on it as a souvenir.

Our love for baseball was intense and we developed strong arms and tanned bodies playing in leagues and in pickup games of football and baseball. On Good Friday in April of 1972, Bobby and I were playing armies with our cousin Jamie at our house. It was not unusual for the older guys to pick on me, but back then I was fearless and would take them on to "prove" myself. From across the yard they had me cornered against a chain-link in the backyard and were throwing mud rocks at me. I was crouched down with a tin garbage can cover as my shield letting them bang away at it, happy that I was small enough to fully hide behind the top so my body was not being hit. During a lull in the barrage, I peeked over the top of the lid and was immediately hit in the left eye. I screamed and they came running over. My eye was numb and I was not yet hurting, but I could not see out of it and that scared me. We went into the car to look in the mirror; it was bruised and yellowing. Jamie said it was time to go home when Bobby determined that he needed to let my dad know. We knew we would be in trouble because, of course, we were repeatedly warned not to throw rocks at each other because we might knock an eye out! By this time, I had snuck up to our bedroom. Our dad took one look at it and said, "we need to go to the hospital." He took me to St. Joseph's. Bobby came along. We waited for what seemed like hours while they tried to locate a doctor. It turned out that they had to page an eye specialist, Dr Keats, who was attending an Astros baseball game. While we waited, a nun was going around the room offering comfort to patients who had yet to be seen. When she came to us and my father told her what had happened, she gave my brother a disapproving look, wagged a finger at him, and said, "God will punish you for that! You should pray for your brother!" While we would look back at this and laugh, at the time he was really worried about the certainty that punishment was forthcoming. When Dr Keats arrived, I was taken to be examined and by this time I was nauseous and dizzy. When he asked me to place my chin on the retinal camera I promptly projectile vomited all over him. Fortunately, he was good-natured about it. My retina was detached and the next morning I had emergency surgery. I shared a room with a young African American about my age who had been shot in the leg. He had been in for several days and was in good spirits. After my surgery I was required to have both of my eyes bandaged for several days, so Bobby was assigned to spend most of those days with me. Although the retina was reattached, I had scar tissue directly across my cornea so since that time I've never been able to see clearly out of that eye and have had several surgeries since then to deal with long-term complications. We never did get punished for disobeying dad's warning about throwing rocks; I think he believed that the aftermath was punishment enough.

My father was wise in ways that I did not come to fully appreciate for years. For instance, when I was in high school my mother and I had a big argument when she thought I had arrived home very late from my after-school job because I was at my girlfriend's house. My mother, and she was not alone in this, had an extensive network of friends who would call her to report sightings of us all over the neighborhood. I am not exaggerating when I say that one afternoon I was just about to get into a fight with several boys who had been taunting me and we were sizing each other up when my mother pulls up and brakes the station wagon and tells me to get in the car! How she arrived that fast, I'll never know, but it is clear that ethnic Mexican families in Denver Harbor functioned like a family, continuing the deep meaningful connections among actual relatives and new friends to support one another—that Treviño noted in Segundo Barrio in the early part of the twentieth century (Treviño, 2006, p. 31). My after-school job at Brookline Rental Company ended at 6:00 p.m. and then I had to run a mile to catch a bus at 6:12 or take another one into downtown and then to Denver Harbor, which took one and a half hours. My other option was to run the six miles home, which I preferred to the slow bus ride. It is true that I would often walk by Cindy's house to see if she was outside so I could say hi. I did so that night but was only there a few minutes. My mother was upset that I was late and began yelling at me. I tried to explain to her that I had run home and she didn't believe me. She was upset and slapped me. I put up my hand to defend myself. She then said I was trying to hit her. This accusation offended me very much. Feeling completely misunderstood, I decided to run away. Of course, I had no money and no real plans. I went to the park and stayed out until about 10:30 that night. I called home and my dad answered. Before I could go into great detail, he said, "tell me where you are and I'll go pick you up. I really need your help; the car has broken down and I need you to help me go get it." We retrieved the car and when we got home, he said, "grab something to eat and go to bed, it's late." Not a word was said about the altercation with my mother, though two weeks later when she and I continued to give each other the silent treatment, he told me to go into their bedroom where she was taking a nap and to not come out until we had spoken with each other. I did as I was told and after several long minutes we did speak to each other and I told her why I was so hurt and upset. She apologized and told me that she loved me. With my voice cracking and tears in my eyes, I did the same. In many respects, I believe that I am more emotionally similar to my mother and this meant that we suffered in silence until it erupted because although we were both highly sensitive, we were not good at expressing our emotions.

Urban renewal, neighborhood warfare, and developing resilience

In the 1960s and 1970s, neighborhood parks were focal points for recreation and urban renewal. Youth summer programs grew out of the Community Action Agencies (CAAs) created by President Johnson's War on Poverty initiative. These programs were designed "to help and encourage children and youth." With names like "Operation Glo" and "Operation PAL (Police Activity League)," the aim of these programs was to develop our minds and bodies through reading clubs and sports activities.[vi] I recall that one summer a local television station did a report on these programs in our neighborhood, and they asked my brother to walk into a portable toilet. I didn't quite understand the concept of him acting for the camera and I tried to follow him. He pushed me back, but they didn't edit that out when it showed on the news and that night everyone got a laugh as they saw it as proof of how much I strived to emulate my older brother. Participation in these programs garnered us T-shirts, free lunch, and a variety of activities and games. At the experiential level, we reveled in the opportunity. But the large-scale urban renewal programs implemented during the 1960s and 1970s, after the departure of the rich and the middle class for America's suburbs, left many inner city neighborhoods more blighted than before as they were part of a larger plan to refine housing segregation practices that supported the development of working-class neighborhoods in proximity to industries that polluted neighborhoods and exposed residents to toxins that stimulated asthma and other respiratory problems.

I realize now that many of those urban renewal public programs I benefited from as a youth were part of the War on Poverty. That was a good war. That was a necessary war, one that still needs to be fought aggressively. As a second-generation Mexican American whose grandparents migrated to avoid the ravages of war in Mexico, I am the product of an ongoing war. As peace activists tried to point out then, and need to point out now, the weapons of mass destruction we faced were to be found here at home in underdeveloped neighborhoods, underfunded schools, the lack of affordable health care for people of all ages, and the list goes on. Born in 1960, my entire life has been marked by conflict at home and abroad. In addition to domestic social movements and rebellions, there were US-led wars and interventions from the Cuban Missile Crisis, the Viet Nam Conflict, the US military interventions in Latin American, the war against Iraq, the war in Afghanistan—the United States has been deploying troops all over the world from Latin America to Asia, to Africa, to south eastern Europe.

I can't help but believe that in my pre-school years I was at least partly bilingual. I don't recall having any communication problems with my grandparents during our visits, even when I occasionally spent several consecutive days there. At home, we spoke English almost exclusively, though my parents spoke Spanish among themselves, particularly when they wanted to hold a private conversation. In our minds, Spanish was a secret language and I think we felt deprived, left out of an inner circle. Though our parents taught us phrases and occasional words here and there, they abided by their purposeful decision to neither teach nor encourage us to speak Spanish, especially once we started school. Many years later, some time in my mid-twenties when I began taking Mexican American Studies courses at the university, I asked them about this rather indignantly. At the time, I was angry at having to, once again, take Spanish in school to recuperate something I felt I should have had as an inheritance if not a birthright. How could they do this to me, I wondered? Didn't they have any idea how embarrassing it was to have to learn Spanish from a gringa, especially when I was surrounded by other Anglos who somehow seemed to have a better grasp of my "native" tongue than me? Though my siblings and I had raised the question before, it was only when we were adults that they gave us some insight into the painful experiences that had shaped their decision. Once we heard their stories, we understood and were able to accept their decision and direct our anger and frustration elsewhere.

I think my parents viewed English language facility, like formal education, as a vehicle of social and economic empowerment. They knew too well from first-hand experience the difficulty and shame that came with trying to unlearn a language and could not see how to create or negotiate an alternative. But our immediate world, defined as it was by the residents of our barrio, was inundated with Spanish in a number of other ways. The little Spanish I knew as an adolescent was more appropriate for street talk, Tex-Mex slang, cuss words, vernacular expressions that expressed our in-group solidarity when needed and which we thought were cool. By and large my youthful world was defined by the boundaries of my neighborhood.

Denver Harbor had experienced an intense case of white flight, but still had many poor Anglo families and elders who were unable to take advantage of suburbanization programs. My brother and I cut the yards of many Anglo widows in our neighborhood, including Mrs. King who lived down the street and gave piano lessons to several of my sisters. I still recall a bully, an Anglo boy a few years older and much taller than me, pushing me around as I walked home from church one day when I was about nine. He knocked me down and kept kicking me, laughing, and taunting me, calling me "meskin" and asking for any money I had. I eventually got up, surrendered the few coins I had, and ran home, too afraid and ashamed to tell my parents what had happened. Despite experiences like this, by and large, this world was ours. Most of us had Anglo friends in the neighborhood with whom we were really close. Bordered by African American neighborhoods, our distinct worlds commingled in limited ways at the park and school.

I will never forget the day that a neighbor across the street David White, his real name, went ballistic for reasons unknown to us, and knocked out a front windowpane and began shooting his pellet gun at anyone in the street, cursing all of us meskins. David was the older brother of Rusty and Lucy, who were good friends with many of us on the block. Some of us lined up down the street from the house to warn others, but none of us thought of calling the police. Instead, someone went to get Joe Yzaguirre. Joe was older than most of us but still in his early 20s. His younger sister Vivian and his little brother Jason often came around to play with the other kids on the block. Joe had a quiet strength and calm about him that made him a natural leader to many of us. Earlier that summer, when Blackie, a neighborhood dog that no one owned but many of us fed scraps to, was hit by a police car speeding down the street that couldn't be bothered to stop and was left fatally injured but still yelping in pain in the street, Joe was the one who came and with sadness but decisiveness finished Blackie off to put him out of his misery. There was no possibility of taking Blackie to a veterinarian. Who would pay? We were all thankful for his mercy and the strength it took to suffocate Blackie. A bunch of us dug a hole in the alleyway to bury our communal pet and Joe gently carried him over and placed him in it so he was not left in the street.

So, when Joe was called on to deal with David, we watched in giddy excitement as he tried speaking to him at a distance, then, when he was met with David's pellet gun and a racist tirade, Joe charged the door at full speed, broke the door in with a kick, and took the gun away from David in a matter of seconds. He dragged him outside and called the police who took a report and arrested David. The Whites moved away soon after that incident and many of us were disappointed to lose Rusty and Lucy as friends.

Interpellation, internalization, and negotiation

In East Texas, perhaps in any part but South Texas where Mexicans have long been a majority and proximity to the border means that Anglos know it's in their economic and political interests to let Spanish and English, Anglos and Mexicans, coexist, if not in harmony, at least in an uneasy truce, whites turned the word Mexican into a dirty word. The purposeful and snide distortion of Mexican into "meskin" was ubiquitous, circulated as it was in movies like John Wayne's *Alamo*. We were the enemy, the inferior, the inarticulate or mute and insignificant others. Though I didn't appreciate it at the time, I think back now of the creative ways in which this linguistic distortion of our identity was deflected. Foremost in my mind is Larry Juarez's reappropriation of this word in public places outside of Denver Harbor where we were a visible minority. Be it in a store, at the Astrodome, or in school, or elsewhere, Larry had a way, embarrassing as it was, of anticipating and taking away the force of this perversion of our identity. In these situations, he would talk loudly and use more Spanish than normal, which always made Anglos nervous, as if we were plotting against them. Most of all he used to like to call out to us, his friends, in an extraordinarily loud voice, "Hey meskin, what you want to do now?" or "Hey meskin, what you want to eat?" It was his way of preempting the sting when it came from them and proclaiming, "yeah we're here" on our own terms. But those terms weren't always under our control.

One Sunday, walking my girlfriend home along the sidewalk after church, an elderly woman began spraying me with her water hose saying, "Get away, get away from my sidewalk, boy." Shocked, I just stayed there, staring at her as Cindy ran out of the way. When I got home, I was soaking wet, and I could not hide my indignity from my parents. I was forced to tell them what had happened. My very angry father drove me back to this house where he threatened to call the police if they dared to do it again. Though they threatened to spray him too, his refusal to tolerate this was an important lesson in self-defense and righteous indignation.

After attending public middle school, I went to a fairly exclusive all-boys Catholic college preparatory school, St Thomas, which was on the other side of town, far from our barrio and bordering

River Oaks, one of the most exclusive neighborhoods in Houston. Life got more complicated there. Operated by the Basilian fathers, St Thomas's motto was: "Teach me goodness, discipline, and knowledge." I learned, or should I say earned, a lot of discipline and knowledge, but not a lot of goodness. A school comprised of what seemed to be more mostly wealthy Anglos at the time, I and the few other boys of color, experienced a lot of hostility and were subjected to lots of humiliation due to racism. Most of the time we suffered in silence. Every once in a while, the violence erupted into a physical confrontation, but most of the time we faced psychological, emotional, and spiritual warfare. And most often we faced it alone as we had little recourse but to internalize it. To be sure, there were times when we projected it onto each other rather than face the force of the majority group's wrath and power.

I'll never forget the first day of high school, my freshman year, when Román Pérez and I were standing next to one another in gym and two guys on each side of us kept pushing us into one another. Scared, not knowing how to speak out or disrupt what was happening, we turned to what was familiar, each other, and started fighting. It was just what these guys wanted—for the two "meskins" to make a spectacle of one another. We had no language to express what was happening to us. We had no social power to leverage our place in this exclusive school; most of us were there on some form of scholarship. So, we internalized this and many other indignities. High school turned me into an introvert. I experienced a profound sense of loss of identity and alienation because I came to despise myself. I became ashamed of my parents, my community, my heritage. I lost my voice.

One day in sophomore year of high school, as we were returning from an off-campus excursion, one of my classmates, a would-be bully by the name of Rocky Mountain, kept pushing me from behind and hurling the word "meskin" over and over, intended as an insult. Afraid of standing up to him because of the school's zero tolerance policy for fights, and cognizant of how angry and humiliated my parents would be if I was expelled, I took his taunts all the way back to the classroom where we received instructions for the next class and were dismissed. As we left the classroom, he did it again, and without thinking, I turned around and, to everyone's shock, including my own, I punched him in the mouth. He immediately started to bleed and looked to the teacher for help. Mr Z, our teacher, who I suspect had seen and heard his taunting, just nodded at us as if to say, go on. Needless to say, we did. But this incident of self-defense did little to alleviate the day-to-day internalization of cultural self-hate.

Being at an all-boys school increased rather than decreased displays of toxic masculinity be this in sports or in the ways discipline was meted out by teachers and coaches. Although it stopped during my time as a student, up until about 1976 school culture allowed one to challenge someone to a fistfight in the gym after school, one that was sanctioned by school officials and often refereed by sports coaches. Those in a duel were required to wear 16-ounce boxing gloves and the rule was that the fight continued until someone gave up. Bloody noses and lips were not uncommon and were accompanied by lots of cheering and jeering from dozens of spectators to this gladiator-like spectacle. Not all fights were official. Some of the more serious fights took place after school off campus without gloves and were equally, if not more, bloody. Somehow, I'm not sure I understand how, this policy of sanctioned fights was permitted to stand alongside a no-fighting rule in which students could be suspended or kicked out of school for fighting others in the hallways or classrooms. It was complemented by intense corporal punishment for infractions perceived by a teacher or coach. These were delivered either on the spot or at a "line-up" after school in which coaches delivered pops to offenders one after the other in a line. Often there was more than one line, and coaches liked to joke about who could make the recipient yelp the loudest when hit. It was, of course, a test of one's manhood to "take it like a man" and not yell when hit. One retired priest, Father Reilly, often served as a substitute teacher. Barrel-chested with a stare that was foreboding and a man of few words, he was known for beginning each class by writing on the board "Time or Meat." In this way, he was democratic and gave you a choice if you misbehaved, either receive pops right then and there or spend time after school in detention. He was legendary for how hard he hit and the small smile this would produce on his face when he did so.

Despite many incidents of racial hostility, I also had several very good Anglo friends. High school was a weird and wonderful time as my world expanded in unforeseen ways. Two of my best friends in high school, Anthony Reilly and Ken Schuler, were steadfast and loyal, often inviting me to their homes. I suppose in some ways we all felt we didn't really fit the mold of the typical St Thomas student. Ken was an athlete, tall and with model looks, and his dad was an agent with A&M records. His parents were divorced, and he could have easily fit in with the obnoxious and elite students at the school, but he was sensitive, open-minded, and curious in ways that they were not. His dad provided a limousine for us to dinner and the prom our senior year. Anthony lived with his oldest sister Liz, who had adopted Anthony as a young teenager when he ran away from home after his mother died. He had come from a large family of 14 and he was also open-minded, and a great storyteller with the most outrageous sense of humor of anyone I had ever known. Anthony and I were roommates for several years after high school, and we shared the experience of putting ourselves through college part-time. He was an actor and through him I got involved in stage productions a few times whenever an extra hand was needed.

High school was also complicated by the typical adolescent growing pains of emotional and sexual maturation. To say these were typical is not meant to undermine mine or anyone else's experiences. Perhaps from reading so much and so widely, or perhaps from my perspective and experiences as a child of a large family, I often embraced a naively idealistic notion of romantic love. From 6th grade until my junior year of high school I had the same "girlfriend." This meant a lot to me, and it filled a need in me to be cared for and be noticed—to matter. Cindy had arrived at Resurrection as a 5th grader, and I immediately found her attractive. I cannot recall how we came to "go together," but I do know that even when I moved on to McReynolds Junior High, I would run the few blocks from there to Resurrection several times a week to carry her books and walk her home one block. We spoke on the phone a lot though in my house a single wall phone made private conversations very difficult, and we would hang out at the park where I played baseball, and she played softball. I tried to be a good, doting, and devoted boyfriend and took her out and gave her gifts when I could, but as we progressed through high school, she began receiving advice from an older cousin of hers that she should date other boys. Despite our adolescent fantasies of a future together, it was not a relationship meant to last. She took her cousin's advice seriously and did end our relationship so she could date other boys. This made me very sad, and in true hopelessly romantic and naive fashion, I wore that sadness as testimony to my depth of feeling for her. In my eyes, love was supposed to last forever, even if it was unrequited and, to my detriment, I tried to prove that I could still remain devoted to her even if she was dating others. Although there were times when we reunited over the next few years, she accepted a marriage proposal when she returned to Houston after graduating from college in San Antonio. Although I wanted us to remain friends, her future husband was jealous and possessive, so we parted ways. Years later when she divorced him, we did reconnect as friends and remain so to this day. While I had convinced myself that genuine love for someone else required self-sacrifice and even sadness, this idealized romantic notion of love was not healthy for me and it was only much later in life that I realized that one must first love oneself in order to receive and reciprocate a healthy love. I would inadvertently undermine a number of relationships in my life because I expected them to leave me, and I accepted and expected relationships to involve heartbreak.

Work and flying the nest

Following my freshmen year of high school in the summer of 1975, I got my first job at the age of 14. Being at St Thomas's made me self-conscious of how little money I had, so a job seemed like a practical solution. One of my classmates, David Rodriguez, learned that I wanted to work and told me that I might be able to get work at Brookline Rental Company, near his house in South Houston off I-45 and Griggs Road. Brookline rented homeowner and contractor equipment, including everything from lawnmowers, floors sanders, sewer cleaning equipment to tractors. I was interviewed very briefly by Pete Hullum, the owner, and given the job on the spot starting at $2.10 an hour. I started there loading equipment and doing basic service and maintenance that involved cleaning and preparing equipment upon return to ready it for the next customer. Pete was only about 30 when I went to work with him, and we got along very well despite the fact that he was something of a country boy having grown up in the small north Texas town of Teague. He liked skimming money off the books, and he would let us work as many hours as we wanted so long as he didn't have to pay us overtime. We would tease each other about race, and I constantly reminded him that he was only successful because most of his customers were non-white and it was they who filled his bank account and lined his pockets with money. In the end, he was good humored and was willing to have his ideas challenged. I worked at Brookline for the next 14 years, initially only on weekends, often in the summer sometimes as much as 66 hours per week, and when I decided not to go to college, a year later at the age of 19, I was made manager of a new store he bought just three miles away from Brookline, Action Rentals, at the intersection of Old Spanish Trail and Griggs Road. Work at either location was hot and dirty, as the buildings were made of sheet metal and only had fans to blow hot air in the shop area. I eventually acquired mechanic skills and drove large gooseneck trailers on tandem trucks as well as a lift bed to deliver backhoes, front end loaders, ditch diggers, and graders.

Having a job that occupied my weekends, including Sundays, meant that I could no longer serve as an altar boy. Having money in my pocket gave me a newfound sense of power. With it, I treated my friends to local restaurants, bought new clothes so I wouldn't have to wear my brother's second-hand clothes, which had been really hard when I was a freshman and he was a senior. A great many of St Thomas's students were very well-off and drove their own cars to school, or were dropped off in BMWs, Mercedes Benzs, Cadillacs, and the like. I was very self-conscious of my dad's mid-70s Pontiac Ventura and often offered to get off the car a block or two away from school, ostensibly so he could save time by avoiding the drop-off line, but really to minimize the embarrassment associated with being in this small economy car. Despite the fact that Denver Harbor was "mixed" with ethnic Mexicans, Anglos, and a few African Americans, I had never felt so self-conscious of my class and race until I went to high school. It was an excellent school for college academic preparation, and I excelled, graduating in the top ten of my class. But in many respects, it was a brutal time for me as I had to deal with overt and covert racial hostility from peers, teachers, and coaches. For instance, I was not allowed to participate in an Advanced Masterworks of Literature class in the eleventh grade despite having better grades than many other students in the class. When I inquired about this, I was told I didn't need it. My parents tried to inquire and were not given a response that made any sense. Coaches would often direct anti-Mexican jokes at students, making us the laughingstock of the class. Despite being an All-Star baseball player and having succeeded so well in the first few weeks of a baseball season in my freshman year that the interim coach kept me on the varsity team, when the regular coach assumed control after basketball season, he eliminated me from not only the varsity team but the junior varsity team too. He told me to not bother trying out the following year. This followed my attempt to play football. To be sure, I was small-framed, but I was fast and a good kicker. Despite this, the coaches assigned me to a guard position, one that required size and strength that was beyond me and predetermined that I would fail. I played the bench the entire year. The football coach was so harsh, racially demeaning, and physically abusive to one of my classmates, David Cavazos, a tall, muscular guy from the Northside who played defensive end, that he hit the coach back one day and a fistfight ensued in which he held his own. He was never seen on campus again. My cousin Paul Hernandez was a student there and excelled in basketball. He was benched and rarely played so he transferred to a public school where he became a starting guard.

While Ken, Anthony, and a few others, like Mr Z (Zarantanello) my cool tenth grade hippie English teacher, did make life at school bearable, I internalized much of what I experienced, and I went from being a confident extrovert to someone who was shy and tried to avoid attention. This inward turn thwarted my dreams and I struggled to imagine a successful career for myself. I did okay at school and graduated well enough to receive scholarships, but in an unexpressed protest against my family, against the educational system, against myself, I refused to go to college. My antagonistic relationship with many peers in high school is substantiated by the *Aquinas,* the yearbook. Editors of the yearbook decided to insert nicknames for each student, and if a nickname didn't exist, they made one up—often one that was degrading. All of the Latino kids who lived in Houston barrios in the north and east end of the city (there were 19 Latino-surnamed boys in all, but about half of those had come from the wealthier Catholic middle schools that served as feeders into St Thomas's) were assigned ridiculous names that mocked their ethnicity like, Amigo, Jack Burrito, El Patio, Viva el Taco, Monteray House (sic), San Antonio, and Padre. Me? I was assigned the name of Slob. To be sure, I was not the best-dressed kid, but I don't believe this assigned slur was about my sense of fashion or comportment. I don't know if the school had faculty or administrator oversight of the student editors, but why they would not or why they chose to allow this, is beyond comprehension. In addition to this slight, in the "official" class group photo my image was blurred. This only exemplified for me how I felt erased and undervalued at St Thomas's. So, at the end of my experience at this elite college preparatory school, all I could ask was, "If this was supposed to be preparing me for college, why would I want to go?" When I received my yearbook post-graduation, I threw it away because it was a stinging reminder of all that I wanted to leave behind.

When I graduated from high school, a small group of us, including Anthony, decided to move into a fabulous, constructed house in the Fourth Ward. This was a three-story brick house that had 11 fireplaces, 22 rooms, and a front room so large one could play handball at either end. It had tennis and basketball courts. Rumors had it that it was Frank Lloyd Wright inspired, but its location in

Image 29 Senior yearbook photo. 1978 Aquinas Yearbook.

Image 30 Graduating class of 1978, St. Thomas High School. I am sitting on bottom row fifth from right. Author's personal collection.

what at the time was an underdeveloped and neglected African American neighborhood meant that few people wanted to live there. We imagined that anywhere from 10 to 15 of us could live there comfortably. I asked my parents if I could move out of our house and this idea was rejected outright. I was told I needed to remain living at home until I was at least 21. I was dismayed with their response. I had finished high school. I had a full-time job. And I wanted nothing more than to be independent. A month later, when my parents and two younger sisters were away from the house on a Sunday, I gathered my clothes and moved out. I was still 17. My parents were upset, especially my father. He spoke with a number of friends and family to try to convince me to go back home. Most of them told him to let me go because I was sensible and mature enough. He went to where I worked and confronted me. He eventually found out where I was living and showed up there. I could not explain it clearly, but I simply no longer wanted to live at home. I was full of rage, sadness, and frustration, and simply wanted to be unfettered. My father did eventually accept my decision and a few months later I received an invitation to lunch at their house. I went and we slowly repaired our relationship.

They may not have expected me to leave the house without going to college or getting married; after all, my dad's brothers were in their 40s and still living with their parents! But they did respect my decision eventually. A few years later when I tried to go to the University of Houston–Downtown for night school, I became very frustrated when my work obligations caused me to miss two midterms in one evening. I stopped going to school and received an "F" in each of those classes because I didn't know about drop/withdrawal policies, and I did not think the teachers would understand. By then, I wanted to get a degree and I was looking for alternatives that would help me achieve this. I explored joining the military and took a test and a physical exam to enlist in the Marines. Two complications arose in that process—one of which saved me from joining. One was that when I received a chest X-ray I was asked if I had ever been shot in the chest. I had to think and finally I remembered being shot in the chest with a pellet gun by Bobby one Saturday afternoon. It had hurt and I had bled a little, but until then I had no idea that the pellet remained within me. Second, I could not successfully pass a vision test because of my earlier eye injury. My inability to do this meant that they could not give me my chosen assignment to work in avionics. When they promised that they would try to accommodate me in something similar after I joined, I declined. Before I learned that I would not join, I went to my parents and told them about my interest in enlisting. They listened and told me that they would support me in whatever I chose to do—that I was my own man. It wasn't until this moment that I truly felt independent. Although I went looking for permission from them, their response made me realize that my life was truly mine. I respected their ability to let me go; they had done their job in giving me as much guidance as possible, and letting me go was a sign of respect and love.

As the manager of Action Rentals, I was responsible for hiring, bank deposits, scheduling workers, and running the front desk. I was also responsible for security after hours. We were located in a higher-than-average crime region of the city and we had an electronic alarm on the building that called the security firm and the police. The security firm would then call me. Pete had armed me with a gun, a .44 Magnum to be exact, so I would be ready to protect his property. Initially, I accepted this charge without hesitation. However, after a number of middle-of-the-night trips to the store where I patrolled the grounds with a gun in my hand knowing that the police might show up any moment and mistake me for a thief with a gun, I told Pete that risking my life was not worth whatever equipment might be stolen. Nor did I think that confronting someone with a gun was the best idea. What was I supposed to do? Shoot someone or hold them captive until the police arrived? We agreed that from that point on I would park nearby and wait for the police to arrive.

I have never been an admirer of guns. I felt that too often the easy access of guns led to shootings and killings that would not have happened otherwise. One incident drives this home for me. Sometime in the early 1980s when I was taking a day off from work and Cindy was home from college, she asked me if I would drive her old Pontiac Sunbird to the dealership so she could trade it in. It was a small sedan, and the dealership was near the Astrodome so I went down Old Spanish Trail to get there. At an intersection near the upper end of downtown, I came to a traffic light stop behind a late model Corvette Stingray that was jacked up in the back. Perhaps the driver thought I almost hit him because with his rear raised I appeared closer than I was, but he shot out of his car yelling at me for being too close to his rear end. I protested and he and his passenger, another big Anglo, came to the side of my car. He quickly punched me in the face several times and began yelling racist epithets at me as his friend tried to open my door, which was locked. I screamed at him that I was going to ram his car, and he ran back to his car and took off. I was so mad, I chased him and gave him the finger. He then let me go around him and began following me. I took off to my place of work and he followed. We pulled into the large driveway, and I ran in and got the .44 Magnum out of the office and ran outside. When he saw me coming out the door with a gun, he sped off. If he hadn't left, I think I would have shot him so full of anger and rage was I at the unjustifiable beating they had given me. I put the gun back up, wrote his license plate number down, and cleaned up my bloody face so I could finish what I had started to do and deliver the car to the dealership. We had a system for obtaining license plate information at work. I located his address and later that night found his car parked outside his apartment. I tossed a bag of sulfuric acid we sold to clean out pipes on his pristine car and left. I am not proud of doing that, but it felt good at the time, and I didn't go to prison for shooting him!

To be sure, as a young man, I did not always know how to channel my frustration and rage with racial aggression and social inequity. My friends and I, like lots of young people of the era, looked for means of escape. Sometimes it was a camping trip where we could let nature decompress us from the stresses of the city life, which often included everyday harassment by police and teachers. Other times, we escaped by simply driving around Loop 610, the highway encircling the inner city, which we called a 610 party. It was not uncommon to drink contraband beer and smoke a few joints. Sometimes our excursions involved driving through River Oaks or Bellaire to see how the wealthy people lived. I recall two specific incidents of class rebellion on our part directed toward those who were better off than us. One time in high school on a Friday night during the Christmas season, Larry, Doug, and I were spontaneously looking at Christmas lights in a well-to-do neighborhood and someone came up with the idea of tying a rope to the outdoor lights decorating the yard to our bumper and taking off. We did it. Another time, we went by a bowling alley in a well-to-do neighborhood and everyone except the driver ran across the tops of an entire row of cars, denting hoods along the way. I don't look back on these incidents with pride; rather it makes me sad that we all had a shared need to act out.

We acted out in other ways as well. This included rolling tires down a tire heap into the path of oncoming cars on Lyons Street then running. When we were younger, my brother and our cousin Jesse used to forage around the neighborhood for aluminum cans or soda bottles to recycle. Soda bottles were like gold because we could get five cents per bottle at the local grocery store. We would work extra hard on Thursday because the local hamburger joint, Dixie Maid, had a two-for-one hamburger and malt special that only required about 50 cents to buy. Movie matinees at the neighborhood theaters, *The Venus* or *The Globe*, cost only 50 cents. We often worked very hard to scrape up enough coins to treat ourselves, but we hit on a scheme that took a shortcut. One of the local grocery stores, Trahan's, stored recycled bottles in a narrowly fenced area behind the store. If we were feeling brave, one of us would be the lookout while one or two of us climbed over the fence and took a case of 24 bottles. Just like that we would have $1.20! We pulled the same move at a Shamrock gas station down the street one afternoon, but we got greedy and were taking turns grabbing cases from behind the station and stashing them in a car wash stall next door when Bobby and Jesse got caught by the owner. I waited for a long time and when they did not come out, I took one case for redemption and went home. It turns out the owner was a retired policeman. He lectured Bobby and Jesse for quite a while and learned why we were stealing empty bottles. He told them that he would give them a dollar whenever they needed it but that if he ever caught them again, he would call the police to have them arrested. Our clever scheme ended that day.

As teens in the 1970s, experimenting with recreational drugs like marijuana, quaaludes, or even LSD was not that unusual. Of course, such behavior was neither condoned nor tolerated by our parents, so we did our best to hide it from them. One Saturday when I was in high school, I came home from work and my father called me into the dining room where he had a joint neatly sliced open on a plate. He asked me if I knew what it was, and I said, "I think it's a marijuana cigarette, dad." To which he replied, "how do you know that?" I said, "well, I've seen it in the movies, and I have seen people smoking in the park." He then proceeded to accuse me of having lost this particular joint. The truth was that there was no way I could have lost it because I didn't have any, and when I did, I rarely took any home. If I did have some, I would often stash it in the garage so as not to take it into the house. He kept insisting that it must be mine, and I protested. He said, "Well, if it's not yours, whose could it be?" I remember rolling my eyes and saying, "How am I supposed to know that? Where exactly did you find it anyway?" "On the sidewalk," was his reply. Well, I said, it could be anyone's! Maybe it was the mailman, or someone just walking down the street." He scoffed in disbelief, and I said, "Look, I know you don't believe me, but that cigarette is not mine. If you were asking me if I have ever smoked marijuana I would have to say yes, but you want me to admit to something that is simply not true, and that's not fair or right, is it?" He raised his eyebrows, gave a smirk, and said, "Ok, I'll let this go but let's be clear that there should be no drugs in this house under any circumstances!"

I said, "Ok, I understand." While it was not unfair of him to assume that it might be mine, it was unfair to insist that it was, so I felt like I won the argument that day based on what was and was not fair. Years later when I was a student in a Chicano Drama class taught by Denise Chavez at the University of Houston, I dramatized this incident in a skit for the class.

My relationship with the church did not end when I stopped being an altar boy. Most of the kids in my family were very active in the CYO (Catholic Youth Organization)—be it playing sports, participating in the choir, talent shows, or recreation camps, the activities and fellowship offered were enthusiastically embraced by all of us. Our parents were more likely to allow us to go to events sponsored by the CYO because of the church affiliation. This, of course, provided us adolescents with good cover to sow our oats in plain sight as there were many co-ed activities. The priests at Resurrection did pay special attention to youth, especially boys, in an effort to keep us out of trouble. We appreciated this but the results were mixed. Father Jack McGinnis was a young priest who hosted a group for boys in which he would sponsor camping trips that often included a broad range of ages, including a number of boys who had already been in trouble with the law. I remember one camping trip to the woods north of Houston where the older guys not only smoked and drank but a few of them went to a nearby house and stole a pig to eat! By the time Father McGinnis found out, the pig was already dead. He reluctantly allowed them to string it up, get it, and cook portions of it, and take the rest home. I don't think these older guys were the role models for us younger ones that he planned on. Another priest, Father Patrick McDonald, left the priesthood to marry one of the teachers at the school. All of the young people liked going to masses held by Father Pat because not only were the songs accompanied by a guitar and tambourines, he would say the mass so fast the service would be over in half the time it usually took. His brother, George, was very influential to a number of family members because of his intense involvement in youth activities and as a music teacher, church pianist, and choir leader. He became my choice as sponsor for my confirmation in sixth grade. Another priest, Father Jim, held sessions with young men in the church rectory. After a while, he would send us to get bottles of wine which he openly shared with us. He taught me how to drive in his light blue VW beetle, and eventually it was he who first introduced me, and a number of others, to marijuana, which he thought got a bad rap from society. He often took us to see midnight movies at the River Oaks Theatre. This was the latest we were ever allowed to stay out since we didn't get home until after 2:00 a.m. or later. I remember one time when I was driving, and we were all partying with beer and weed when a cop pulled me over for a wrong turn. Father Jim immediately put on his priest collar and said we should let him do the talking. I didn't have a license yet, but he managed to talk us out of trouble by explaining that he was spending time with these poor inner-city youth who needed guidance and structure to their lives. They let us go and we left with him at the driver's wheel. Later that summer, he left the church when he was suspended for including a diatribe during a church service in opposition to legal restrictions against marijuana when it did no real harm. I never heard from him again. I am fortunate that despite these hippie priests and others like Fr Wendland who were stern and severe (grumpy), I was not aware of ever interacting with a priest who sexually abused children in our parish. I do know that Houston-Galveston diocese was not immune from these incidents but neither I nor anyone I know, as far as I am aware, ever encountered this.

When we were young, my siblings and I listened to the Top 40 hit parade together on Saturday mornings. Mary Ann, Bobby, and Beabee used to practice dance steps together while Margie and I pranced around. I remember us teaching each other dances like "The Hitch Hike," "The Swim," "The Locomotion," and "The Hustle." In high school in the late 1970s, I often felt you had to choose your social circle by the music you liked. For us, it was a hard and fast choice between disco music or rock and roll. I was rock and roll all the way! We also learned to dance Tejano to cumbia, polkas, and ranchera music. My mother loved listening to rancheras and boleros but mostly on her own. We danced to Tejano music at quinceñeras, weddings, and anniversary celebrations where we learned by trial and error and watching others.

We were not afraid to work. Bobby had a job as a dishwasher, a newspaper route, and he excelled at selling garden seeds. In high school he worked as a delivery boy at a posh high-rise off San Felipe Drive. It was a job I inherited from him when he graduated from high school. In addition to working at Brookline, I also worked at Weiner's Department Stores as a stocker. One summer in high school I was working three jobs at a time. My parents required that we give them some money that went toward paying tuition at St. Thomas's. If we did not do this, we would have been obliged to answer phones at the priest rectory after school to pay for a portion of our tuition. I also worked as a grocery bagger and loader at Jamail's luxury supermarket off

Kirby Drive. It was owned by the uncle of one of my classmates. I was fired one day for supposedly talking too much to him while we waited for customers to come through the line. My friend protested but was promptly told to go take a break while they made sure I left the store immediately.

Police confrontations: compliance and resistance

In May 1977, near the end of my junior year in high school, Houston was riven by news of the death of José Campos Torres, a Viet Nam veteran, at the hands of Houston police. His body was found floating in Buffalo Bayou on 8th May where he was thrown after a severe beating on 5th May by police, following an arrest at a local bar on drunk and disorderly conduct. He was so severely beaten that the jail intake sergeant refused to admit him. Officers were told to take him to a hospital for medical care but that was the last time he was seen. As Veronica Guzmán Hays and other scholars have shown, violence at the hands of law enforcement is part of a pattern that goes back to the beginnings of the Texas Republic (1995).[vii] Growing up non-white in Texas one learned, especially men of color, that every interaction with a police officer was potentially dangerous, so while I, like many, was appalled to hear of the brutality of Campos's killing, I was not surprised. What was most surprising was to think that the police might actually be held accountable for their egregious violation of Campos's rights.

Being stopped, frisked, and verbally harassed by police was routine. This was true not only in Houston but anywhere in Texas, and it was probably true throughout the South. I recall drives to

West Texas in the '60s where we stopped at restaurants where we could only buy food to go. We were stopped by police on the highway for no reason other than a state trooper wanting to check my father's driver's license. My father was always highly deferential to police, saying "Yes, officer" and never questioning why he was stopped. Within Houston the stops were intense everywhere throughout the city. If you dared asked what was wrong, the typical answer was, "There has been a report of a stolen car just like this one in the area." I once expressed my experiences through a poem.

La Chota

Getting stopped by the police
(a.k.a. la chota)
in East Houston was as certain
as humidity on a hot summer afternoon.

We learned to see the underneath
a raging red tempest of
resentment against the
red, white, and blue lights
in our rearview mirror.

No way to win.
Complain? Risk elevating
the situation to a physical confrontation-
your word against theirs-
a vacation behind bars for sure!
Run? At least a beating,
perhaps an underwater excursion

in a local bayou with
handcuffed wrists.
A sure recipe for death.

Taking it
meant learning your place
when a cop says:
what, YOU a student?
When all I have is a university ID and
I had to be lying.

You're expected to know
that frisking is their special way of saying hello and

> *that being meskin*
> *is probable cause*
> *enough to pull you over...*
> *for being brown in H-town.*
> — From *A Journey Around Our America* (2012)

The six police officers involved in José Campos Torres's killing were put on trial and convicted of negligent homicide and were sentenced to one-year probation and a $1 fine. On May 7, 1978, weeks before my high school graduation and a day shy of the one-year anniversary of the discovery of his body, a riot/rebellion occurred at Moody Park in Houston's northside at a Cinco de Mayo celebration. One of the organizations leading the rebellion was People United to Fight Police Brutality (PUFPB), an offshoot of the local chapter of the Revolutionary Communist Party (RCP). Activists Travis Morales, Mara Youngdalh, and Thomas Hirschi were arrested and faced trial as instigators of the riot.

Seven years later, as a student activist at the University of Houston, I would meet Travis Morales and attend several meetings of the RCP with fellow students. Although we backed off from being active members of the RCP because we felt that they were too radical for us and were seeking opportunities for conflict with the police, we formed a coalition with them for a couple of years, particularly on the issue of immigrant justice and the emergence of privately-owned immigrant detention centers. In particular, Corrections Corporation of America, one of the nations' largest, had just opened facilities in the Houston area and a coalition began protesting at their sites to draw attention to the need for immigration reform.

Between two worlds: searching for a meaningful life

Our parents wanted us to be safe, self-sufficient, and protected from racial hostility. Despite this, they could not protect us from the animus we experienced based on the color of our skin and our last name. These made us visible targets for unwanted attention and gave rise to a whole host of conflicted feelings about ourselves, our culture, and our place in the world. Don't get me wrong here. Our parents were not ashamed of being *mexicano,* nor did they teach us to be. Their social, political, and cultural outlooks were formulated in a period now characterized as the Mexican American generation.[viii] They believed in self-advocacy and self-reliance. They believed they could simultaneously be proud of their Mexican heritage and be good US citizens. In this way they negotiated the terms of their daily existence as they sought to improve the quality of their lives and create opportunities for their children that they never had. Our culture, as everyone's, was integrated into our daily lives in our religion, music, food, extended familial relations, the way we were taught to honor the living and the dead, and many other customs we practiced. And this culture was integrated within, not apart from, baseball, hotdogs, rock 'n' roll, the fascination with the exploration of space, in a time when the world around us was changing rapidly in the context of the civil rights movement, the women's movement, and the assassination of brave leaders of change. During these years of transition following high school, I embraced short-term fulfillment and sought escape even though I felt a need to find a larger purpose for my life.

Following high school, my late teens and early 20s were all about working hard and partying harder. In my initial effort to discover myself, drinking and drugs were an everyday occurrence. No doubt there was pleasure, but it also became routine and unfulfilling as I realized I was biding time in the hope that life would somehow take a turn for the better. My life was divided by the work and recreation with my friends from Denver Harbor, and my small circle of Anglo friends from St. Thomas's. It was often disorienting to attend theater performances or concerts in the early part of the evening and then go and party hard with my friends in Denver Harbor. I loved both sets of friends, but they were like oil and water and I could not envision a future in which they would intermingle. In a two-year period between the ages of 19 and 21, I was arrested twice for public intoxication, one time while driving home from my cousin Jesse's wedding and once on 4th July 1980 when a group of us were fishing overnight on a drawbridge between the mainland and Galveston, Texas when the police suspected one of us of obstructing train traffic but without knowing who, arrested all six of us. It was then that I began to think seriously about what options getting a degree might provide.

I recall explicitly one weekend night, after I had been hanging out with Anthony and Ken and other friends, going to catch up with a group of my other friends and, as I was late to the party, I realized that they were all high on acid and they were having a bad trip. There was ugly sniping at each other and the threat of violence lingered. I left because there was no joy in being there. I also told myself that I needed to find a way to give my life more meaning and coherence. It wasn't until several years later when I began taking a small engine mechanics class at a local community college that I remembered how much I liked to read and learn. It took me almost seven years going to school part-time and working 50 plus hours a week to get my BA, perhaps because I was a part-time student, but also because I couldn't decide on a major. Finally, when I was 25, my life was profoundly impacted by the first Chicano literature class I ever took. Here, for the first time in 1985, did I realize "we" had a literature and began to contextualize and connect our struggle for survival and cultural preservation.

Although I started and stopped taking college courses several times at Houston Community College, UH-Downtown, and San Jacinto College, it wasn't until my rejection from the Marines that I decided I needed to change my life—and that meant prioritizing school over work. In 1985 I resigned my position as manager of Action Rentals and agreed to work only part-time, 36 hours a week. I had been attending school without focus and kept exploring different majors—I initially tried courses in Computer Science, Accounting, Business, because I thought I should pursue courses that would lead to a lucrative career, but I found the subject matter boring. I finally allowed myself to prioritize what gave me pleasure and fulfillment, which was reading and writing, so I decided to major in English. One semester I signed up for a Mexican American literature class with Tomás Vallejo and I was hooked. I could not believe how easily I related to the stories, novels, and poems of Evangelina Vigil Pinon, Raúl Salinas, Tomás Rivera, Rodolpho Anaya, and others. Writing about them was an opportunity to discover who I really was and where I came from. It validated my life experience.

My ultimate decision to study English and Mexican American Studies was guided by imagination and passion. Reading literature had always offered me a way to broaden my basis of experience, to free myself from constraints and limitations of the real world, and to understand that the world was much bigger than my family, and neighborhood. In short, it both broadened my horizons and served as a form of escapism. But in Chicano literature I saw ways to understand the grandeur and the human struggle for existence that made my life, our lives, equally important, equally provocative, and rich with philosophy, metaphysical quests for meaning, as well as love, pain, and desire.

I transferred from UH-Downtown to UH-Central because after this Chicano literature class I was hungry for similar courses. I found them in the Mexican American Studies program at the Central campus. In my first class with Lorenzo Cano called "The Barrio" I found a framework to understand where Denver Harbor fitted in with Houston's political economy. In Mexican American sociology and history classes, taught by Tatcho Mindiola and Emilio Zamora, I read scholarship by Mexican Americans that reordered my worldview and began to give me the tools and knowledge to regain my voice so I could speak back. Faculty in those classes showed me that education could be personally and socially empowering. They helped me develop as a human being who felt he had something to say and something meaningful to offer others. My Chicana/o professors treated me like I was important, like *my* life story and *my* dreams and ideas were worth listening to. I began to feel less insignificant and more responsible for making a difference. Critical thinking, literature, and writing gave shape to my emerging cultural, social, and political awareness.

An early credo I learned was the idea that "the more you know, the more you owe." This emerging sense of social obligation that goes hand in hand with knowledge made me even more thirsty to find a way to make a difference.

I met a number of peers who became lifelong friends and who would eventually also become powerful scholars and teachers. Among these are Sandy Soto (from South Houston), Ben Olguin (from Magnolia Park), Freddy Porras (North Houston), Tom Carrizal (East End), and Hector Gonzalez, to name but a few. While there was one student organization at the time, MASO (Mexican American Student organization), which was mostly a support and social group. When I started going to school full-time, I loved the interaction with peers outside of class, but I wanted more, so I started a Chicano student discussion group, which was intended to bring students together to identify and discuss what we considered the most pressing issues impacting the well-being of the Mexican American community. We held several successful discussions but wanting to do more, this served as a catalyst for launching an organization we initially called Hijos del Sol out of respect for our pre-Colombian heritage. A strong feminist, Sandy steadfastly challenged this until we changed it to Hijas and Hijos del Sol and then to MEChA. Under the group we began printing our own newspaper addressing what we considered pressing social issues. Chief among these was police harassment and immigrant justice. We sponsored rallies, developed coalitions, and went on the local public radio station to magnify our message. During this time, The United Farmworkers Union launched a second national campaign to boycott grapes. Through Texas UFW organizer, Rebecca Flores, we joined that cause and had the opportunity to meet César Chávez. As an activist and advocate for a number of causes, I worked to transform my sense of self by speaking at public rallies, attending marches, and expanding my knowledge of Chicano Studies, public policy, and various forms of leadership and advocacy. In other words, I reclaimed my lost voice.

When I completed my BA in the winter of 1987, I had no clear idea where I was going. I gave serious consideration to joining the Peace Corps in the spring of 1988. I thought that if I joined and went to Latin America, it might give me a chance to immerse myself in Spanish and finally become fluent. I drove to Dallas, took a test, and received an interview. During the interview I expressed my interest in being assigned to Latin America but when I received an offer it was only for places in the Middle

Image 31   Grape Boycott Campaign workers, Cesár Chávez, Sandy Soto, myself and others,. circa 1986. Author personal collection.

East. I declined and when I asked why I wasn't given my top choice, I was told that they were concerned that I might have too much interest in the region because of my background. This was the late 1980s and there was political unrest in Guatemala, El Salvador, and Nicaragua. I have to admit that I did care, and I knew enough to be critical of US policy in Latin America. After my failed attempt to join the Marines, I had been relieved that I did not do so because I later learned that unlike the Peace Corps the military sought to recruit more Latinos to join to assist in their Central American intervention efforts. It was after this failed attempt that I began seriously exploring options like teaching in high school or pursuing an MA After exploring the Peace Corps and considering an application to a high school English teacher position, one of my former English professors at UH, Erving Rothman, encouraged me to apply to graduate school. Ignorant about the dynamics of admission, I sought letters from faculty and drove to the University of Texas in Austin in mid-March to hand deliver my application. It was the only school to which I applied. I was fortunate to get accepted in late May.

Sandy decided to continue her undergraduate degree at UT-Austin, where her mother had been a student. So together we headed out to Austin. At the age of 28, all I knew was that I carried within me a love for Chicano literature that had begun to help me understand my life in relationship to others. In many respects my pursuit of a graduate degree was a continuation of my effort to discover myself and to find, not a profession, but an authentic and meaningful purpose for my life that would allow me to not only self-advocate but to contribute to building a better world.

There is, of course, more to my story, including the continuation of my education and growth as an activist, and my role as a professor. But that story will be continued elsewhere.

Coda

I left Houston behind even though it had recently undergone numerous changes for the better. With the 1981 election of Kathy Whitmire, we had not only Houston's first female mayor but Houston's first African American police chief and a leader who sought to advocate for the equality of women and ethnic and sexual minorities.

According to a 2018 report by the Kinder Foundation, Houston is one of the most diverse metropolitan areas in the country. It has a population that is more than a quarter foreign-born and 44 percent Hispanic, according to 2016 estimates from the census.[i] Leah Benovitz, the author of "Within Houston's Diversity, A Complicated Story Still Being Told" notes that, "For young people and newcomers to the city, it can be hard to picture the Houston that once was. In the 1940s, the city had just under 600,000 people, according to census estimates. The schools were segregated and so were many of the neighborhoods."

To be sure, the spatial, racial, and sexual politics of Houston have shifted over the years. The first African American mayor was elected before the end of the century, and the current mayor is African American and in his second term. Annise Parker, elected in 2010, was one of the first openly gay mayors of a major US city. Although Joseph Jay "J. J." Pastoriza was elected as Houston's first Hispanic mayor in 1917, he died after only serving in office for three months. Since then, no other Latino has been elected. Nor has an Asian American ever served as mayor.

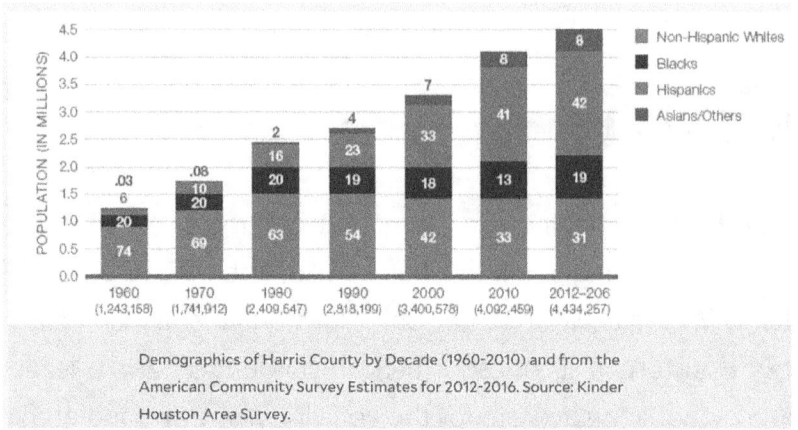

Figure 1 *Kinder Survey. Reprinted by permission of* Kinder Houston Area Survey / Kinder Institute for Urban Research.

The window into politics and power offered by the identity of elected officials in Houston notwithstanding, it is clear that Houston is no longer the typical southern town that it once was. Its identity has been remade by major demographic change and a deeper understanding that its diversity is actually an asset that can be leveraged economically and politically. While it is not the same city rife with segregation and a cowboy mentality that I grew up in, it still has far to go to become a truly equitable place to live.

In this book I have shared the story of the Mendoza-Martinez family as a lens through which we could understand the growth and well-being of Houston's Latina/o population. I started with the premise that my family's story paralleled the story of the ethnic Mexican population in Houston. According to a 2022 report on Houston Public Media, Hispanic Texans now comprise the largest demographic group.[ii] The same is true in Houston. One cannot discuss the Latino population in Houston without also discussing the internal diversity of that community, for no longer is it sufficient to discuss only people of Mexican descent. No up-to-date and reliable source of disaggregated data on Houston's Latino population is extant, but it should be noted that the vast majority are of Mexican descent even though there are a significant number of other Latinos present in the Houston Metropolitan Area, including Puerto Ricans, Central Americans, Cubans, and South Americans.

The political temperature of Texas and the USA at large means that Latina/os everywhere in the state continue to be intensely racialized and they face choices about who they wish to be and what vision of the United States they wish to embrace. As I believe I have demonstrated in this book, these are not easy or even free choices, although I believe one can more readily participate in a non-hegemonic life that was once possible. The picture I have portrayed of ethnic Mexicans in Houston mostly focused on two neighborhoods, Magnolia Park and Denver Harbor. I cannot pretend that what I have portrayed represents all neighborhoods nor that my experience is emblematic of all Latinos, but what I have shared is a genuine part of the larger picture.

We are not a perfect community. Magnolia and Denver Harbor are not to be idealized nor held up as shining examples of utopian communities. There was poverty, inter- and intracultural violence, domestic frictions, structural racism, systematic underdevelopment and neglect, as well as the emergence of gangs that preyed on the weak or those seeking connection at any cost. Nevertheless, I believe that ethnic Mexicans in Houston have survived and even thrived over the generations even as its community has been renewed with new immigrants from

Mexico and elsewhere. As is true for communities all over the country, strong communities are made up of strong families, of strong kinship, and friendship networks that support one another in times of duress and personal and collective economic or social pressures. What has enabled the survival and success of members of these neighborhoods is community resilience, the ability of some segments of the residents within those neighborhoods to withstand, adapt to, and recover from adversity by organizing and acting collectively on behalf of their individual and collective betterment in the face of structural violence—be it a difficult job market, police harassment, political underrepresentation, inferior schools, or internecine battles. These are lessons to be learned and from which to glean and hone strategies to not only survive, but to thrive. Among these are the benefits of a strong work ethic, social, political, and cultural arts organizations, cultural retention, formal and informal networks of care, an ability to be bilingual and bicultural, and an ethic of reciprocity and mutuality.

Although we have long since moved away from Denver Harbor and the houses on Hoffman and Zoe in which my family was born into and raised, it was a place that sustained, nurtured, and served as a site of learning for not just my family, but relatives, dear friends, and other residents who once lived or continue to live there. The landscape continues to change. Threats and opportunities continue to abound. Some see it as a place to leave, a sign of mobility when one does. Others see it as a place to draw lines and resist policies that threaten neighborhood well-being.

The very nature of history is that change occurs over time, and I believe Houston has changed for the better by becoming more accepting of its multiethnic population. This story was meant to not only document and bring to the surface my family's story, but my wish is that it will also resonate for others even though there will be points of divergence. As I hope I have made clear, I believe the Latina/o population has much to contribute to developing a stronger economy, stronger neighborhoods, and a stronger society if we but find that common ground steeped in love for family, perseverance, and the pursuit of justice.

Notes

Prologue

i. A note on the use of ethnic identifiers for people of Mexican descent and Latina/os is necessary here. Many years ago, in his important essay, "On Culture," Chicano historian Juan Gómez Quiñones noted that an ethnic name dance occurs among non-white people in the United States because the ethnic identifiers reflect power, ideology, and identity of the in-group users and outsiders. In colonial Texas, Texian refers to Anglo settlers within Mexican Tejas and those Anglos who advocated for Texas's independence from Mexico. Mexicanos generally refers to Mexican nationals, but it can also refer to immigrants from Mexico within the United States. Tejanos refers to people of Mexican descent who have lived within Texas long enough to identify it as their homeland. They are generally born and raised in Texas and retain a certain amount of ethnic pride associated with their Mexican heritage. Hyphenated Americans, such as Mexican-Americans (without or without the use of an actual hyphen) are US citizens of Mexican descent who still identify with Mexican culture as part of their heritage. This term became popular in the 1930s during an intense time of Americanization in which it was necessary to assert one's legal status and nationality in a period in which outsiders or perceived foreigners were being maligned and targeted. Racialization of immigrants, cultural outsiders, and those with different phenotypes than the dominant population has existed throughout the history of European occupation of the Americas (García, 2000). The ethnic name game can be used to build community among people with shared ethnic and linguistic traits. It can also be used to separate, distinguish, and dominate perceived outsiders.

ii. For a profile of second-generation immigrants, see www.pewresearch.org/social-trends/2013/02/07/second-generation-americans.

iii. See Daniel Morales's "*Tejas, Afuera de México* (2021)."

Introduction

i. This data is taken from the World Population Review online database: worldpopulationreview.com/us-cities/san-antonio-tx-population.

ii. The treaty was later abrogated and Mexico only formally ceded lands north of the Rio Bravo when the Treaty of Guadalupe Hidalgo was signed ending the US-Mexican War in 1848. See Griswold's *The Treaty of Guadalupe Hidalgo* for an excellent overview of the aftermath of the treaty.

iii. While not strictly adhering to their style of blending history and creative non-fiction, Gay Talese's *Unto the Sons* (1992) and Alaina Roberts's, *I've Been Here All the While: Black Freedom on Native Land* (2021) were inspiring examples of authors who blended historical and literary narrative to tell their family's story. I would be remiss to neglect mention of authors like Alejandro Morales, Victor Villasenor, Emma Pérez, and Norma Elia Cantu, among others, who masterfully blend history and fiction.

1 Fragments of the past: on family genealogy as a mosaic

i. For an excellent overview of Americanization, see Paul's encyclopedia entry (2018) on this topic provided in the list of References.

ii. This poem is titled "El Amor Filial." A copy of it was found in "Parnasso Lirico Escolar," a book of school songs and poems compiled by José Zurón. I am deeply grateful to Elena Méndez for identifying the source for me.

2 Becoming Americans: surviving, negotiating, and thriving under acculturation

i. Much of this information is derived from three sources: (1) An interview with Zapopan Martinez conducted by her son Joe Martinez, her daughter Dora Martinez, and her daughter-in-law, Lily Martinez circa early 1990s; (2) interviews with my parents conducted circa 2011; and (3) an interview with my aunt Dora, aka Sister Patricia conducted on 11/12/2022 at her retirement home in San Antonio.

ii. The Texas State Archives website states that the 1925 drought set an 86-year record for high temperatures and low rainfall in a single year. See also "Major Droughts in Modern Texas: A Cycle of Drought and Flood" (2022).

www.tsl.texas.gov/lobbyexhibits/water-droughts

iii. www.chron.com/news/houston-texas/article/Podunk-Texas-It-s-not-far-from-Houston-1812379.php

iv. Pachucos are Mexican American youth of the mid-twentieth century who participated in a counterculture that embraced zoot suit fashion, jump blues, jazz and swing music, and spoke a caló dialect. Among Mexican Americans it was most common in the Southwest and was widely seen as an idiosyncratic form of rebellion against the constraining conventions of their parents' generation.

v. In the late 1980s when the hotel was closed, they sold furniture to the public. Joe and Mary went and purchased two lounge chairs, had them re-upholstered and they sat in their den for many years.

vi. For an advanced discussion of how Mexican American identifier emerged in a time when they were forced to strategize within the Anglo-American binary racial order and with the monoracial imperative, see Daniel G. Reginald's essay (2022).

vii. www.chron.com/local/history/economy-business/article/Character-builder-Houston-s-zoning-battles-8342526.php

viii. In Shelley vs. Kraemer Supreme Court Chief Justice Fred Vinson ruled that the Fourteenth Amendment's Equal Protection Clause prohibits racially restrictive housing covenants from being enforced. For the last 25 years there has been a statewide effort to abolish language in documents.

ix. Other examples may be found here: www.npr.org/2021/11/17/1049052531/racial-covenants-housing-discrimination. Accessed March 19, 2023.

x. For fuller discussion of Operation Wetback, see Kelly Lytle Hernandez's work.

3 Coming of age in the Space City: cowboys, astronauts and other specters

i. https://z-upload.facebook.com/BullockMuseum/posts/10160394830231096

ii. See Brian McTaggert for the history behind the Astros' team name.

iii. See www.sciencedaily.com/releases/2021/06/210614110824.htm

iv. See "When interstates paved the way: the construction of the interstate highway system helped to develop the US economy" for a detailed analysis. www.richmondfed.org/publications/research/econ_focus/2021/q2-3/economic_history

v. www.strongtowns.org/journal/2017/2/20/the-history-of-urban-freeways-who-counts. Also see Herriges (2017) for a more detailed analysis of the impact of interstates on communities.

vi. The 1960s marked a period of significant expansion in PAL's educational programs. Head start pre-school was initiated in 1964. President Lyndon B. Johnson launched the "War on Poverty" in 1963, and federal funds were allocated for PAL and other youth-oriented programs (Phelps, 2014).

vii. See *Brown Bodies and Police Killings: The Case of José Campos Torres, Jr and Anti-Mexican Violence in Texas in the 1970s* for an extensive study of the impact of this event on Houston.

viii. See Mario Garcia's, *Mexican Americans: Leadership, Ideology, and Identity, 1930–1960*.

Coda

i. https://kinder.rice.edu/urbanedge/within-houstons-diversity-complicated-story-still-being-told

ii. www.houstonpublicmedia.org/articles/news/texas/2022/09/15/433078/hispanic-texans-may-now-be-the-states-largest-demographic-group-new-census-data-shows/

Recommended projects, assignments, and discussion questions

Discussion questions

1. What limitations or "blind-spots" result from a top-down historical approach? What challenges might be encountered with telling history from the bottom up? Do you think that the stories of everyday people matter, or should our study and knowledge of the past focus on political leaders and other movers and shakers? Why or why not? Discuss the relationship of minority and working-class histories with "official" master narratives. Are they easily reconciled or are they incongruous? Explain.
2. Can you see the role that social identities (race/ethnicity, gender, sexuality, etc.) have played in city planning where you grew up? Provide examples.
3. What gaps are there in your family history? What do you wish you knew about your ancestors? Why is this information not easily accessible? How does your family discuss its own past? Is it something to be learned from or as something to

be left behind? Is your familial past seen as a touchstone for how much life has gotten better or worsened?
4. What value and/or limits, if any, do you see in familial stories?
5. While official history is often shaped by formal documents such as those that articulate policies or laws, or the interviews, memoirs, and journals of important leaders, how do we understand the role of everyday folks in history? What evidence might "everyday experience" bring to the table? What insights or expertise can they offer to historical events? What insights might personal letters, high school paraphernalia, memory books, and other ephemeral matter provide for helping to reconstruct one's life story as part of a larger narrative? Can these materials provide insight into individual lives in the larger context of national and regional events?

Recommended projects

Create a genealogy map or family tree chart if you don't already have one.

Think of items you or family members possess that could provide insight into your life. Assemble a few and tell a story that situates the powers of these items in a particular pace and time.

Assignment

Write a 500-word essay on the lessons or values you believe you can learn from ancestors previous to your parents.

Construct a timeline of key formative events of your life that could serve as a foundation for your life narrative.

Bibliography

AsoMexFFCC. Derechos de Paso Vigentes en el Sistema de Ferroviario Mexicano. Early 20th Century train routes from Mexico City. Rail transport in Mexico. Available at: https://en.wikipedia.org/wiki/Rai l_transport_in_Mexico. Created 25 April 2014. (Accessed March 19, 2023)

Babinck, M. 05/10/2007. *Houston Chronicle*. Available online at: www.chron.com/news/houston-texas/article/Podunk-Texas-It-s-not-far-from-Houston-1812379.php. (Accessed July 1, 2023)

Beeth, H. & Wintz, C. D., eds. (1992). *Black Dixie: Afro-Texan history and culture in Houston*. College Station, TX: Texas A&M University Press.

Benjamin, K. (2003). Progressivism Meets Jim Crow: Curriculum Revision and Development in Houston, Texas, 1924–1929. *Paedagogica Historica*, 39(4), 457–476. Available at: https://doi.org/10.1080/00309230307476 (Accessed February 11, 2022)

Binkovitz, L. (04/18/2023). "Within Houston's Diversity, A Complicated Story Still Being Told." Rice University Kinder Institute for Urban Research. Available at: https://kinder.rice.edu/urbanedge/within-houstons-diversity-complicated-story-still-being-told. (Accessed January 11, 2023)

Boney, J.L. (2021). NO Blacks Allowed!!! *Forward Times*. Available at: https://forwardtimes.com/no-blacks-allowed/ (Accessed October 13, 2022)

Bullock Texas State History Museum. (2022). Posting on Facebook commemorating 62nd anniversary of desegregation. Available at: https://z-upload.facebook.com/BullockMuseum/posts/10160394830231096. (Accessed July 2, 2023)

Bryant, S. (2016). Mexican Americans and Southwestern Growth. [online] Digital History. Available at: www.digitalhistory.uh.edu/disp_textbook.cfm?smtID=3&psid=597 (Accessed September 11, 2022)

Calderón, Roberto. *Mexican Coal Mining Labor in Texas and Coahuila, 1880–1930*. College Station, TX: Texas A&M University Press.

Castillo, C. (2022). Interview with Louis Mendoza. Zoom.

Cardoso, L. A. (1980). *Mexican Emigration to the United States, 1897–1931*. Tucson, AZ. University of Arizona Press. Available at https://doi.org/10.2307/j.ctvss3xzr\ (Accessed September 15, 2022)

Chapman, B. (2007). "Houston went through peaceful segregation movement in secret." Houston Business Journal. Available at: www.bizjournals.com/houston/stories/2007/01/22/newscolumn1.html. (Accessed April 10, 2022)

Cole, T.R. (1997). *No Color is My Kind: The Life of Eldrewey Stearns and the Integration of Houston*. Austin: UT Press.

Contreras, R. (2021). Mexican Inclusion and Exclusion in Houston Texas from 1900-1940. M.Ed. University of Houston, College of Liberal Arts and Social Sciences.

Cortinas, M. (2022). Interview with Louis Mendoza. Zoom.

Cutler, L. (2006). "Salon Juárez." *The Houston Review*, [online] 3(2), pp 36–37. Available at: https://houstonhistorymagazine.org/wp-content/uploads/2014/03/salon-juarez.pdf (Accessed July 14, 2022)

Daniel, G. R. (2022). From Multiracial to Monoracial: The Formation of Mexican American Identities in the US Southwest. *Genealogy*, [Online] 6(28). Available at: https://www.mdpi.com/2313-5778/6/2/28 (Accessed December 9, 2022)

Davis, E. A. (2004). *How the Antioch Missionary Baptist Church in Houston, Texas between 1945–1954 Facilitated the Educational Development of Soldiers Returning from World War II: A Historical Analysis*. ProQuest Dissertations Publishing. University of Houston.

De León, A. (1989). *Ethnicity in the Sunbelt: A History of Mexican Americans in Houston*. University of Houston Series in Mexican American Studies 4. Houston: Mexican American Studies Program, University of Houston.

Demographics of Harris County by Decade (1960–2010) and from the American Community Survey Estimates for 2012–2016. Source Kinder Houston Area Survey/Kinder Institute for Urban Research.

DePillis, L. (07/05/2015). "Character Builder: Houston's Zoning Battles." Houston Chronicle. Available at: www.chron.com/local/history/economy-business/article/Character-builder-Houston-s-zoning-battles-8342526.php. (Accessed January 19, 2023)

Dressman, F. (1987). Visions for Houston: Booster Literature, 1886–1926. *The Houston Review*, [online] 9(3), pp 137–154. Available at: https://houstonhistorymagazine.org/wp-content/uploads/2014/06/visions-for-houston-booster-lit-HR-9.3.pdf (Accessed June 16, 2022)

El Tecolote. [Advertisement of a baseball game, Alamos versus Magnolia Park] Poster, March 21, 1931. Available at https://texashistory.unt.edu/ark:/67531/metapth221921/ (Accessed March 20, 2023), University of North Texas Libraries, The Portal to Texas History, with permission from Houston Metropolitan Research Center at Houston Public Library.

Esparza, J. J. (2011). La Colonia Mexicana: A History of Mexican Americans in Houston. *Houston History* (*Special Issue: Houston: Nuestra Historia*), [online] 9(1), pp. 2–8. Available at: https://houstonhistorymagazine.org/wp-content/uploads/2012/03/Esparza-La-Colonia-Mexicana.pdf (Accessed February 5, 2022)

Fregoso, R. (2002). *Bronze Screen: 100 Years of the Latino Image in American Cinema*. Minneapolis: University of Minnesota University Press.

García, M. C. (2000). Agents of Americanization: Rusk Settlement and the Houston Mexicano Community, 1907–1950. In: E.

Zamora, C. Orozco, and R. Rocha, eds., *Mexican Americans in Texas History: Selected Essays*. Austin: Texas State Historical Association, pp. 128–137.

Garcia, M. (1991). *Mexican Americans: Leadership, Ideology, and Identity, 1930–1960*. New Haven: Yale University Press.

Garza, N. (2011). The "Mother Church" of Mexican Catholicism in Houston. *Houston History (Special Issue: Houston: Nuestra Historia)*, [online] 9(1), pp. 14–19. Available at: https://houstonhistorymagazine.org/wp-content/uploads/2012/03/Garza-Mother-Church.pdf (Accessed May 22, 2022)

Gómez-Quiñones, J. "On Culture." (1977). Issue 1 of UCLA-Chicano Studies Center Publications, Popular series, no. 1.

Gornick, V. (2002). *The Situation and the Story: The Art of Personal Narrative*. New York: Farrar, Straus and Giroux.

Griswold, R. (1992) *The Treaty of Guadalupe Hidalgo*. Norman: University of Oklahoma Press.

Greene, C. (1988). Guardians against Change: The Ku Klux Klan in Houston and Harris County, 1920–1925. *The Houston Review*, [Online] 10(1), pp. 3–20. Available at: https://houstonhistorymagazine.org/wp-content/uploads/2015/12/10.1-kkk-.pdf (Accessed July 6, 2022)

Guillen G. D. (2019). "Some Houston Deed Restrictions' Language Still Restrict Certain Races." *Houston Chronicle* [online] Available at: www.chron.com/neighborhood/homes/article/Houston-deed-restrictions-race-home-size-language-14108562.php (Accessed July 12, 2022)

Guzman Hays, V. (1995). *Brown Bodies and Police Killings: The Case of José Campos Torres, Jr and Anti-Mexican Violence in Texas in the 1970s*. Master's Thesis. Texas A&M University, Corpus Christi. Available at: https://tamucc-ir.tdl.org/bitstream/handle/1969.6/89231/Hays_Veronica_thesis.pdf?sequence=1&isAllowed=y. (Accessed January 5, 2023)

Hadley, N. (1991). Harbor, Industry, and Homes. *The Houston Review*, [Online] 13(1), pp. 35–48. Available at: https://houstonhistorymagazine.org/wp-content/uploads/2014/02/13.1-Harbor-Industry-and-Homes-Nancy-Hadley.pdf (Accessed June 22, 2022)

Harris, J., McGrew, J., & Huhndorff, P. (1989). *The Fault Does Not Lie with Your Set: The First Forty Years of Houston Television*. Fort Worth, TX: Eakin Press.

Haynes, R. (1976). *A Night of Violence: The Houston Riot of 1917*. Baton Rouge, LA: Louisiana State University Press.

Hernández, K. L. "The Crimes and Consequences of Illegal Immigration: A Cross-Border Examination of Operation Wetback, 1943 to 1954." *Western Historical Quarterly* 37, no. 4 (2006): 421–444. https://doi.org/10.2307/25443415. (Accessed November 16, 2022)

Herriges, D. (02/21/2017). "The History of Urban Freeways: Who Counts?" Strong Towns. Available at www.strongtowns.org/journal/2017/2/20/the-history-of-urban-freeways-who-counts. (Accessed January 17, 2023)

Hirschman, C. & Mogford, E. (2009). Immigration and the American Industrial Revolution From 1880 to 1920. *Social Science Research*, [online] 38(4), 897. Available at: https://doi.org/10.1016/j.ssresearch.2009.04.001 (Accessed September 16, 2022)

Historical Population: 1900 to 2017 City of Houston (Source: US Census Bureau 1900–2010).

Hollem, H. R., photographer. "Mexican Cotton workers in fields near Corpus Christi, Texas circa 1930s." United States. Office of War Information. Available at www.loc.gov/ (Accessed March 19, 2023)

Houston Facts 2021. Available at: www.houston.org/sites/default/files/2021-09/houston%20facts%202021_digital (Accessed February 7, 2022)

Jackson, S. (1980). Slavery in Houston: The 1850s. (publication name illegible) [online] pp 76–82. Reginald Moore Sugar Land Convict Leasing System research collection, MS 636. Woodson Research Center, Rice University, Houston, Texas. Available at: http://archives.library.rice.edu/repositories/2/archival_objects/298198 (Accessed February 25, 2023)

Kellar, W. (1996). "Alive with a Vengeance: Houston's Black Teachers and Their Fight for Equal Pay." The *Houston Review*. Vol 18. Available at: https://houstonhistorymagazine.org/wp-content/uploads/2014/02/18.2-Alive-With-A-Vengeance-Houstons-Black-Teachers-and-Their-Fight-for-Equal-Pay-William-H-Keller-.pdf. (Accessed November 6, 2022)

Kleiner, D. J. "Magnolia Park." Texas State Historical Association. Available at www.tshaonline.org/handbook/entries/magnolia-park-tx. (Accessed April 7, 2022)

Kreneck, T. H. (1981). The Letter from Chapultepec. *Houston Review*, [online] 3(2), pp. 267–271. Available at: https://houstonhistorymagazine.org/wp-content/uploads/2014/02/3.2-The-Letter-From-Chapultec-Thomas-H-Kreneck.pdf (Accessed June 22, 2022)

Kreneck, T. H. (1989). *Del Pueblo: A Pictorial History of Houston's Hispanic Community*. Houston, TX: Houston International University.

Kreneck, T. H. (1985). Documenting a Mexican American Community: The Houston Example. *The American Archivist*, [online] 48(3), pp. 272–276, 278–285. Available at: www.jstor.org/stable/40292917. (AccessedJune 22, 2022)

Licea, B. (2022). Interview with Louis Mendoza. Zoom.

Lima-de-Oliveira, R and Fux, J. (2014). Speculative History. *Olho d'água*, [online] 6(1), pp. 67–77. Available at: www.olhodagua.ibilce.unesp.br/index.php/Olhodagua/article/viewFile/249/232 (AccessedSeptember 18, 2022)

Major Droughts in Modern Texas: A Cycle of Drought and Flood. Texas State Library and Archives Commission. Available at: www.tsl.texas.gov/lobbyexhibits/water-droughts. (Accessed August 9, 2022)

Robert K. Nelson, LaDale Winling, Richard Marciano, Nathan Connolly, et al. "Mapping Inequality," *American Panorama*, eds. Robert K. Nelson and Edward L. Ayers, Available at: https://dsl.richmond.edu/panorama/redlining//#loc=12/29.746/-95.444&city=houston-tx (Accessed March 20, 2023)

Martinez, P. (2022). Interview with Louis Mendoza. San Antonio, Texas.

Martinez, Z. (circa 1990). Interview with Joe Mendoza, Lilian Mendoza, Sister Patricia Martinez. Houston, Texas.

McCaa, R. (2003). Missing Millions: The Demographic Costs of the Mexican Revolution. *Mexican Studies/Estudios Mexicanos*, [online] 19(2), pp. 367–400. Available at: www.jstor.org/stable/10.1525/msem.2003.19.2.367 (Accessed September 7, 2022)

McComb, D.G. (1969). *Houston: The Bayou City*. Austin: University of Texas Press.

McTaggert, B. (2021). The History Behind the Astros' Team Name. Available at: www.mlb.com/news/houston-astros-team-name-history. (Accessed anuary 1, 2023)

McWhorter, T. (2011). Trailblazers in Houston's East End: The Impact of Ripley House and the Settlement Association on Houston's Hispanic Population. *Houston History* (*Special Issue: Houston: Nuestra Historia*), [online] 9(1), pp. 9–13. Available at: https://houstonhistorymagazine.org/wp-content/uploads/2012/03/mcwhorter-Ripley-House.pdf (Accessed September 7, 2022)

Mendoza Family Archives. Numerous letters, memory books, photos, birth and death certificates, school records, and other memorabilia were made available by the children of Joe and

Mary Mendoza as a resource for this publication. These are now owned by many of them and stored in their homes.

Mendoza, G. "Zapopan (1998). Tribute poem to Zapopan Martinez upon the occasion of her funeral service.).

Mendoza, J. and Mendoza M. (circa 2011). Interview with Louis Mendoza. Houston, Texas.

Mendoza-Trostmann, G. (2022). Interview with Louis Mendoza. Zoom.

Mendoza, R. (May 12, 2022). Interview with Louis Mendoza. Zoom.

Mendoza, L. (1988) Unpublished essay on "Being Hispanic in Houston."

Mendoza, L. (1998). "Zapopan" Unpublished poem.

Mendoza, L. (2005). "Lengua Americano, Corazon Chicano: Finding a Lost Voice in America." *Telling Tongues: A Latin@ Anthology on Language Experience.* Austin: Red Salmon Press.

Mendoza, L. (2012). *A Journey Around Our America: A Memoir on Cycling, Immigration, and the Latinoization of the United States.* Austin: University of Texas Press.

Mendoza, L. (2003). *Historia: The Literary Making of Chicana and Chicano History.* College Station. Texas A&M Press.

Mindiola, T. (2015). Houston. In *Oxford Bibliographies.* Available at: www.oxfordbibliographies.com/view/document/obo-9780199913701/obo-9780199913701-0021.xml. (Accessed November 23, 2022)

Morales, D. Tejas, Afuera de México: Newspapers, the Mexican Government, Mutualistas, and Migrants in San Antonio 1910–1940 Journal of American Ethnic History (2021) 40(2), pp. 52–91.

Morales, D. S. and Schmal, J. P. (2004). How We Got Here: The Roads We Took to America. [online] Houston Institute for Culture.

Available at: www.houstonculture.org/hispanic/roads.html (Accessed June 6, 2022)

Muñoz Martinez, M. (2018). *The Injustice Never Leaves You: Anti-Mexican Violence in Texas.* Cambridge: Harvard University Press.

Murguia, A. (2002*). The Medicine of Memory: A Mexican Clan in California.* Austin: University of Texas Press.

Paul, C. (2018). "Americanization." Virginia Commonwealth Social Welfare History Project. Available at: https://socialwelfare.library.vcu.edu/programs/education/americanization/. [Accessed September 11, 2022)

Pasztor, S. (1994). *The Spirit of Hidalgo: The Mexican Revolution in Coahuila 1910–1915.* Doctorate. University of New Mexico.

Phelps, H. "When Interstates Paved the Way: The construction of the Interstate Highway System helped to develop the US economy." *Economic Focus.* second / third quarter, 2021. Available at: www.richmondfed.org/media/RichmondFedOrg/publications/research/econ_focus/2021/q2-3/economic_history.pdf. (Accessed February 2, 2023)

Phelps, W.G. (2014). *A People's War on Poverty: Urban Politics and Grassroots Activists in Houston.* Athens, GA: The University of Georgia Press.

Prewitt, S.W. (1995). *Everything from Ditch Diggers to Doctors: LULAC Council 60, a Mexican American Civic Organization in Houston, Texas, 1945–1960.* MA. University of Houston.

Pruitt, B. (2013). *The Other Great Migration: The Movement of Rural African Americans to Houston, 1900–1941.* Vol. 21. Sam Rayburn Series on Rural Life. College Station, TX: Texas A&M University Press.

Pruitt, B. (2005). "For the Advancement of the Race: The Great Migrations to Houston, Texas, 1914–1941." *Journal of Urban History,* [online] 31(4), pp. 435–478. Available at: https://doi.org/10.1177/0096144204274394 (Accessed 7, 2022)

Reginald. D.G. (2022). "From Multiracial to Monoracial: The Formation of Mexican American Identities in the US Southwest." *Genealogy* 6: 28. Available at: DOI: 10.3390/genealogy6020028. (Accessed January 18, 2023)

Rhinehart, M. D. and Kreneck, T. H. (1988). "In the Shadow Of 'Uncertainty': Texas Mexicans and Repatriation in Houston During the Great Depression." *The Houston Review*, [online] 10(1). pp. 21–33. Available at: https://houstonhistorymagazine.org/wp-content/uploads/2014/06/shadow-of-uncertainty-HR-10.1.pdf (Accessed November 8, 2022)

Rinehart, M. D. and Kreneck, T. H. (1989). The Minimum Wage March of 1966: A Case Study in Mexican-American Politics, Labor, and Identity. *The Houston Review*, [Online] 11(1), pp. 27–44. Available at: https://houstonhistorymagazine.org/wp-content/uploads/2014/02/11.1-The-Minimum-Wage-March-of-1966-A-Case-Study-in-Mexican-American-Politics-Labor-and-Identity-Thomas-H-Kreneck-1.pdf (Accessed April 9, 2022)

Rodriguez, A. M. (2018). Antigone's Refusal: Mexican Women's Reponses to Lynching in the Southwest. *The Journal of South Texas*, 31(2), pp. 44–76.

Rodriguez, N. (2000) "Hispanic and Asian Immigration Waves in Houston." *Religion and the New Immigrants: Continuities and Adaptations in Immigrant Congregations*. Eds. H.R. Ebaugh and J S. Chafetz. Walnut Creek, Calif.: AltaMira Press.

Rogers, S. (2016) "The Maps and Loans Behind Houston's Segregation." *Houston Chronicle*. Available at www.houstonchronicle.com/local/gray-matters/article/Redlining-Houston-9970251.php. (Accessed December 8, 2022)

Rosaldo, R. (1994). Cultural Citizenship in San Jose, California. *Political and Legal Anthropology Review*. [online] 17(2), pp. 57–63. Available at: (www.jstor.org/stable/24497930) (Accessed October 27, 2022)

Rosales, F. A. (1981). Mexicans in Houston: The Struggle to Survive, 1908–1975. *Houston History Magazine*, [online] 3(2), pp. 224–248. Available at: https://houstonhistorymagazine.org/wp-content/

uploads/2014/02/3.2-Mexicans-in-Houston-The-Struggle-to-Survive-1908-1975.pdf (Accessed June 15, 2022)

Rosales, F. A. (1985). Shifting Self Perceptions and Ethnic Consciousness among Mexicans in Houston, 1908–1946. *Aztlan: A Journal of Chicano Studies,* 16(1–2), pp. 71–94.

Rosas, M. (2022). Interview with Louis Mendoza. Zoom.

Sadasivam, N. (2018). "How Anglo farmers brought an end to Latino ranching in the Rio Grande Valley." Quartz. Available at: https://qz.com/1353805/how-anglo-farmers-brought-an-end-to-latino-ranching-in-the-rio-grande-valley (Accessed January 10, 2023)

Sadowsky, S., (2018). A Short History of the Cotton Industry in Travis County. [online] Historic Preservation Office. Available at: www.austintexas.gov/edims/document.cfm?id=307020 (Accessed July 9, 2022).

Salazar, J. (2021). *Mutiny of Rage: The 1917 Camp Logan Riots and Buffalo Soldiers in Houston.* Amherst, NY: Prometheus Press.

San Antonio, Texas Population 2023. Available at: worldpopulationreview.com/us-cities/san-antonio-tx-population. (Accessed July 17, 2022)

San Miguel, G. Jr. (1991). "The Community Is Beginning to Rumble": The Origins of Chicano Educational Protest in Houston, 1965–1970. *The Houston Review,* [online] 13(3), pp. 127–147. Available at: https://houstonhistorymagazine.org/wp-content/uploads/2014/02/13.3-The-Community-is-Beginning-to-Rumble-The-Origins-of-Chicano-Educational-Protest-in-Houston-1965-1970.pdf (Accessed October 14, 2022)

San Miguel, G. (2001). *Brown, Not White: School Integration and the Chicano Movement in Houston.* College Station, TX: Texas A&M University Press.

Sánchez, A.R., Hernández, F., Briante, S., Bringas, E., Clement, J., Ramírez, M.G., Ramón López V. et al. "ZACATECAS." *Artes de México,* no. 34 (1996): 73–88. Available at www.jstor.org/stable/24326624 (Accessed August 19, 2022)

Sanchez, G.J. (1995). *Becoming Mexican American: Ethnicity, Culture, and Identity in Chicano Los Angeles, 1900–1945*. New York: Oxford University Press.

Santillán, R. A., et al. (2017). *Mexican American Baseball in Houston and Southeast Texas* (Images of America). Arcadia Publishing.

Santos, J. P. "The Secret History of the Texas Rangers." *Texas Monthly Magazine*. June 2020. Available at: www.texasmonthly.com/arts-entertainment/secret-history-texas-rangers/. (Accessed November 17, 2022)

Second-Generation Americans: A Portrait of Adult Children of Americans. Pew Research Center. Available at: www.pewresearch.org/social-trends/2013/02/07/second-generation-americans/ (Accessed3 July 13, 2022)

Sepulveda, R. (2022). Interview with Louis Mendoza. Zoom.

Schuetz, R. A. (2019). Decades-Old Deed Restrictions on Race Still Found in Texas. [Online]NBC DFW. Available at: www.nbcdfw.com/news/local/decades-old-deed-restrictions-on-race-still-found-in-texas/136483 (Accessed December 11, 2022)

Simons, H. and Hoyt, C. A. (1992). *Hispanic Texas: A Historical Guide*. College Station, TX: University of Texas Press.

Spencer, D. (2005). "Mexican Migration to the United States, 1882–1992: A Long Twentieth Century of Coyotaje." Presentation at the Research Seminar Series of the Center for Comparative Immigration Studies at the University of California, San Diego, September 27, 2005, Working Paper.

Steptoe, T. L. (2016). *Houston Bound: Culture and Color in a Jim Crow City*. Oakland, CA: University of California Press.

Struthers, S. (2012). La Iglesia Nuestra Señora de Guadalupe celebra 100 años. *La Voz de Houston*, [online] Available at: https://

web.archive.org/web/20120819133943/http://www.lavoztx.com/news/2012/aug/17/la-iglesia-nuestra-senora-de-guadalupe-celebra-100/ (Accessed August 6, 2022)

Susaneck, A. P. (2018). Segregation by Design: Houston. [online] Segregation By Design. Available at: www.segregationbydesign.com/houston/redlining. (Accessed January 4, 2023)

Svetaz, M.V., Coyne-Beasley, T., Trent, M., Wade, R. Jr., Ryan, M.H., Kelley, M., and Chulani, V. (2021). The Traumatic Impact of Racism and Discrimination on Young People and How to Talk About It. In: *Ginsburg, K. R., editor and Ramirez McClain, Z.B., associate editor., Reaching Teens: Strength-Based, Trauma-Sensitive, Resilience-Building Communication Strategies Rooted in Positive Youth Development*, 2nd edition. Itasca, IL: American Academy of Pediatrics. pp. 307–328.

"Texas Forever." 1836 Advertisement for land to new settlers in Texas. Briscoe Center for American History. Texas Broadside Collections, file photo 73.93

"The East End: Then and Now." *East End Houston*. Available at: https://eastendhouston.com/the-east-end-then-and-now/. (Accessed September 15, 2022)

The Texas Population Project. "Population Growth in Texas, 1850–2000." Available at: https://texaspolitics.utexas.edu/archive/html/cult/features/0501_02/slide1.html (Accessed March 7, 2022)

Treviño, R. R. (2006). *The Church in the Barrio: Mexican American Ethno-Catholicism in Houston*. Chapel Hill, NC: University of North Carolina Press.

Ura, Alex. (09/15/2022). Hispanic Texans may now be the state's largest demographic group, new census data shows. Houston Public Media. Available at: www.houstonpublicmedia.org/articles/news/texas/2022/09/15/433078/hispanic-texans-may-now-be-the-states-largest-demographic-group-new-census-data-shows/. (Accessed January 5, 2023)

Von der Mehden, F.R. (1984). *The Ethnic Groups of Houston.* Houston: Rice University Studies.

Wimberly, C., Martinez, J. Munoz, D., and Cavazos, M. "Peons and Progressives: Race and Boosterism in the Lower Rio Grande Valley, 1904–1941." Available at: The Western Historical Quarterly 0 (Winter 2018): 1–27. doi: 10.1093/whq/why094 (Accessed October 19, 2022)

Zamora, Emilio. (1993). *The World of the Mexican Worker in Texas.* College Station, TX: Texas A&M University Press.

Zurón, J. H. "El Amor Filial." *Parnaso Lirico Escolar.* (1966) Ariston Press. Tegucigalpa, D. C., Honduras. C. A. (24).

Index

affirmation 71, 134

Americanization xxi, 11, 38–39, 74, 98, 197

anti-Mexican 198

barrio 4–5, 175

belonging xxiii, 123

citizenship 3, 12, 30, 38, 47

civil rights 70, 108, 116, 172

Coahuila xxv, xxviii, 22–24, 54, 75

community xviii, xxiii, xxx, 5, 7–8, 12, 33, 35–37, 39, 42, 52, 58, 70–72, 76, 98, 106, 112, 149, 174, 176, 183

cotton 10, 20, 25, 27, 36, 51, 54, 58, 75

Denver Harbor xxii, 7, 81, 98, 101, 111–112, 127–128, 130, 138, 141, 145, 148, 155, 173, 175, 183

deportation xxi, 70

displacement xviii, 31

identity xv, xvii, xxiii, 7–8, 13, 71, 121–122, 148–149, 182

immigration

migration 171

Magnolia

Magnolia Park. 7–8, 11, 35–39, 46, 49, 53–54, 67, 71–73, 75, 79, 81–82, 84, 87, 92, 99, 101, 106, 176, 183

memoir. xv, 13, 119

memory. xv, xvii, xix, xxiii, xxiv, xxv, 8, 10, 113, 123, 194

migrate. xxxi

oil. 10, 22, 34, 43, 46, 93, 173

Parras. xxv, xxviii, 20, 42–43, 45–46, 50, 84, 86

police. 109, 122, 146–148, 160, 162, 164, 168, 170–171, 173, 176, 181

racism

racialization. 3, 32, 39, 71, 149

redlining. 11, 81, 99–101

revolution

Civil War. 22–23, 137

Rusk Settlement House. 35, 38, 57, 70, 77

Second Ward
  Segundo Barrio. xxviii, 5, 26, 34–37, 46, 53
segregation. 34, 38–39, 41–42, 71, 182
Ship Channel. 6, 58
Southwestern. 105
Space City. 13, 119, 121

urban renewal. 143–144

violence. 10, 23, 28, 30, 97, 109, 149, 168, 173

work. xx, xxi, 4–7, 13, 15, 18, 20, 23–24, 26, 35, 37, 43–44, 46–47, 51–55, 58, 61, 75–76, 84–85, 87, 94, 96, 99, 105, 107, 119, 126, 133, 154, 159, 161, 163–164, 167, 173–174

www.ingramcontent.com/pod-product-compliance
Lightning Source LLC
Chambersburg PA
CBHW070801230426
43665CB00017B/2441